Khaled Bassyouny is a six languages multi-lingual plastic surgeon of African-Egyptian roots, he's a remarkable athlete, a talented musician, a loving husband, and a father of two.

He was inspired to write *The Tongue Chains* by his decades of experience as a proud stutterer, his autobiography serves as double-edged sword, an intriguing, unusual story, a worldwide eye opener on an issue always ignored by the public as well as an insight resonating with people who stutter along with non-stutterers all over the world to continue pursuing their dreams.

Stutterers and non-stutterers.

Khaled Bassyouny

THE TONGUE CHAINS

A Stutterer's Odyssey

AUSTIN MACAULEY PUBLISHERS™

LONDON • CAMBRIDGE • NEW YORK • SHARJAH

Ordering Information
Quantity sales: Special discounts are available on quantity purchases by corporations, associations, and others. For details, contact the publisher at the address below.

Publisher's Cataloging-in-Publication data
Bassyouny, Khaled
The Tongue Chains

ISBN 9781647507657 (Paperback)
ISBN 9781647507640 (Hardback)
ISBN 9781647507664 (ePub e-book)

Library of Congress Control Number: 2023900569

www.austinmacauley.com/us

First Published 2023
Austin Macauley Publishers LLC
40 Wall Street,33rd Floor, Suite 3302
New York, NY 10005
USA

mail-usa@austinmacauley.com
+1 (646) 5125767

A friend and proof-reader: M. Hamed.

He was a six-year-old boy the first time he was in jail, prosecuted by his once called best friend, then forever swapped to become his worst enemy; he was a joyful kid enjoying playing with his wooden pistol while making new friends. He was loved by his family and close ones. Nevertheless, so clueless about what this jail will represent to him when he grows up, his name is Khaled, and this is his story.

I was born twice: first, as a baby boy, on the sacred hot lands of Cairo, Egypt in May 1987; and then again, as a teenage boy on the verge of suiciding far away from my home country on the cold lands of Ukraine, in August 2007. Surviving wasn't easy, especially when Taurus was there; I have always been told to hide my abilities, but what's the use? crossing oceans, overcoming mountains, and meeting different mentalities is what forged me into what I am today, in a span of 30 years I got bent, punched, cut, split, riveted and welded back, just to be able to defeat Taurus, but is it enough?

I have always believed that my story could be a reason for someone's inspiration, but if you really want to know it, the first thing you'll probably need to know is where I was born, and how my lousy childhood was like, and how my parents were occupied and all before they had me.

Chapter 1
The Dream

On a sunny November Monday, the air was cold, and the wind was strong. I could feel the hairs on my body raise as the cold wind hit my face as I sat on a swing in the local playground. Small children were playing on the various, colorful play equipment as their parents kept a watchful eye on them. The noise of dogs barking at each other playfully as they chased each other in circles almost drowned out the cries of a baby whose mom was too busy talking to her friends to notice the baby had lost its dummy.

With fallen leaves all over the place, you'll find me right there by the soccer field looking at a group of boys playing a soccer match.

"Hi, can I play with you?"

"No, we're much older than you, go away."

"But please, I don't have any other friends."

"Go and play with someone your age!"

I went to sit with my family, watching my grown-up parents talking with their grown-up friends about grown-up stuff; my father introduced me to his friends.

"This is Khaled, my son, he has an invisible friend, isn't that cute! Khaled, say hi to Uncle Sam."

I greeted him and then went back to the soccer field, walking slowly with hands in my pockets, when a voice in my head told me.

"You can make them win; you're a good runner."

I smiled.

"Hey guys, if you let me play for your team, I'll make you win; I am a fast runner."

(Silence)

They looked at each other and mumbled some words I couldn't hear.

"Okay, you're in," they said.

I was the youngest kid on the field, I don't even know what made them believe me, but they did.

I scored a goal that day, and we won that game. They picked me up happily, asking me if I could come every Saturday to play with them again, I was overjoyed that I earned their trust.

That voice in my head, I don't know what it is and where is it coming from, but it had always accompanied me, pushing me to trust myself in the first place and convincing others that I am superior. Since birth and at times when I felt I wasn't good enough. It always came out when I needed it.

I used to stand up for small kids getting bullied in the playground, against boys double my size, where they literally can break me into pieces; hearing that voice inside of me telling me that I can do anything, it didn't allow me to be afraid, no matter who and what is in front of me.

I loved it, at all times, it was the source of my confidence and my best friend. I was six years old.

We were a happy family of five living in a not-so-big apartment in Abu Dhabi, Emirates. Me, mom, dad, and my two brothers, I was the middle one.

I rarely spent time with my father, him being always at work but always there on the weekends trying to make things up. He was a hard worker who always dreamed of having a big family and maintaining a certain living standard.

My mother was managing her time perfectly, just like a typical middle-eastern mother, being a full-time mom of three boys, starting from waking up earlier than all of us every morning, preparing breakfast for us before school, and for dad before going to work, dropping us at school and taking us back, feeding us after school, helping us in our homework, by the time my dad gets back from work, dinner was already ready on the table, we eat together, then she put us to sleep after telling us a bed time story.

I always wondered how can she do all of this and still maintain her duties as a wife, but she did it flawlessly.

While being the middle brother, my relationship with my brothers was and always have been strong, we were raised in a way to always love and care for one another and to have each other's backs as we grow older.

I came home one day from playing hide-and-seek with my friends in the alley, as I fell and got myself bruised, I was rushed by my over worrying mom to the hospital emergency room, it was my first time in a hospital.

On a plastic hallway chair I sat, legs kicking in the air, clearing the floor by several inches as they swung back and forth. The doctor was mesmerized by my red rubber boots on my feet and my blue duffle coat, I probably reminded him of Paddington Bear. My face looked scared and had that unhealthy look to it, and my eyes were hard to open as I stared at nothing on the wall. The doctor approached, my legs weren't swinging in the carefree way he'd first assumed. Each one was more like a kick, sharp and pointed. He crouched down in front of me, letting me see his white coat and stethoscope, and brushed his blonde bangs from his face. "Hey there, I'm Doctor James. What's your name?" I became still and was quiet for a moment, sitting further back into the chair.

"Khaled" came out almost like an accident, spilling out of my drawn inward lips. My brown eyes lost their harshness, becoming rounder, more glossy. Then all at once, my face buckled, my breathing stopped momentarily, and tears streamed.

In an attempt to calm me down, he chatted with me about school and friends while checking on my vitals one more time. I liked the way he kept on calling me "boss" even though I clearly wasn't the one running the show here, his speech was peppered with humor, and throughout it all, he never frowned or let his face fall in seriousness or judgment, then with a flourish he pulled a penny from behind my ear, then another and another.

The doctor had me lie on my stomach. Next, he examined the inflamed muscle in my left lower back.

"I'm going to inject Novocain into that injured muscle," said the doctor to the nurse, right before he brandished that weapon of a hypodermic needle.

He laid the extra-long needle right beside me on the table. I looked away at the wall, trying not to center my attention. However, my eyes swung back to it as if out of control. The tube with the medicine never grew. But the needle desired to be thrust into my poor innocent back, which never harmed anyone.

The needle grew fast like the Hulk grows when he is angry. The doctor came back and plunged that needle into the sore place when the doctor released the medicine, blessed relief! All the pain left.

"Are you okay?" asked the nurse.

I said, "Piece of cake."

I stepped out of the emergency with a smile; that scene was almost like a vision to me since then; as I waved goodbye to the doctor, I saw myself in a typical cabinet someday.

I used to lay my head on my pillow every night in silence, listening to my inner voice telling me how proud he is of the bravery I showed in the hospital, a best friend who kept on narrating to me how we'll conquer the world when we grow up, until I fall asleep.

But that Tuesday night was a little different. By the time I went to bed to get early for school the next morning, he didn't say anything.

"Kids, it's sleep time," my father said.

My sandwich had one last bite when I said, "But Daddy, I don't want to sleep now; I want to sit with you and mom!"

"It's already late son, go to your room, turn off the light and go to sleep, you have school tomorrow."

"Can I sleep with the lights on, Daddy? I don't like the dark, I am afraid."

"No, son, you're a big boy now, you're old enough to sleep with the lights off," he insisted.

It was my first night to sleep in the dark.

I entered my room and turned off the lights; it's only the moonlight that's shining the room now; I laid my head on the rounded pillow of my two floors bed, my elder brother is sleeping above me, and I am trying hard to go to sleep but I can't. My best friend was silent, and my eyes were refusing to fade into sleep.

That Friday night, as soon as I closed my eyes, my brain started to hibernate. I had a feeling of numbness in my body, trembles all over my head, my whole head was fluttering, and I had that strong urge to open my eyes, but I couldn't.

With the moonlight shining in my room, I managed to forcibly open my eyes, however, I wish I didn't.

A big black figure appeared from the window, his face wasn't clear, so shadowy, I wouldn't see any of his features, so ominous and mysterious, slowly he started approaching me, the closer he gets, the more my head wobbles. I wish I was able to wake up. I couldn't even scream; I wanted all of this to end, I don't want to sleep in the dark anymore, I wanted to run and hide behind my father. But I was helpless, I couldn't move, I had my first sleep paralysis, it was like I was in chains, tied all the way down to the ground, I was numb, without a single movement.

I feel this blackness lay over me. Like a blanket, but not a blanket of warmth but a blanket of coldness making me shiver, somehow, it's making my eyes feel heavier and heavier.

The figure was reaching out for my ears, he whispered. "Sr-s-srt-"

He muttered some words I can't remember, a mumble that wasn't clear due to my panic and head moving convulsively.

The voice was unexpected. It was low, with an agreeable trace of huskiness and with a hint of more power than the frail body would suggest; his voice was rasping, like an old man, even though his shadow reflection looked young.

The apparition was no more than a distortion of the light, a human cut out of colors. As he moved, the things behind him appeared bowed, as if I looked at him through a mild fish-eye lens. Then as quickly as he came, he left, without leaving so much as a foot impression in the fall mud.

Suddenly the trembles stopped, I closed my eyes once again, and the figure went back to where it came from. I slept the whole night without any other abnormalities.

"Good morning, sweetheart, go wash your face and eat your breakfast."

The buzzing sound of the radio in my ears, playing the channel my mother used to listen to every morning.

My mother dropped me at school.

"Have a good day, sweetheart."

I remained speechless for two days.

My mom finally received a call from my school that I refuse to speak.

Not a single word.

On the 3rd day, my mother woke me up to school.

"Good morning, sweetheart, are you okay today?"

"GGGGood morning, Mmom."

I started speaking again, and I regained my normal life. However, the words didn't seem to come out fluently; there was something wrong, having no idea what is that and

17

where did it come from; I had my stutter since then, and it was there where my journey to fluency started.

Chapter 2
Cataclysm

"Dad, wake up, you promised me shawarma today," I said while tickling his big feet on a Saturday morning.

"From which part should I start eating you, you little duck," he says upon waking up.

He tickles me, picks me up, and throws me in the air like he always does; at the highest point of the throw, I pause for fragments of seconds before I come back to his strong arms, almost two meters above the ground, during these parts of seconds I used to experience many feelings, adrenaline mixed with trust that he won't let me fall, knowing that he will re-catch me when I get back down. This always remained as one of my most Innocent moments of happiness as a child.

I choose the most perfect memory of my father and cling to it. I choose it because at that moment; he was the person he should have been, would have been, had it not been for the stress of life. In that snapshot, his unwarped personality was something so golden and sacred I want to keep it forever. Like an old movie reel, I can play it at will; it's already summer, in the backyard of our old house. He's laughing, relaxed after washing his car. He asks me if I would want a wooden pistol for my next birthday; of course I do, when did a six-year-old doesn't?

In moments, he has my right wrist and ankle. He spins like a shot-putter, but he never let's go. The backyard turns into a blur; I'm flying, flying until he can spin no more. The memory has no smells or weather other than a lack of rain. The garden is in fine detail, the crab apple tree, the rhododendron bush, the weeds in the flower beds. But the finest detail is his face, creased with love and my joy, not only for the ride but for being with him, for being with my dad.

As a kid, I loved shawarma so much that when my parents asked me what do I want to be when I grow up.

"A shawarma man" was always usually my answer.

I used to always ask them.

"Is there a school for shawarma guys?"

"What grades should I get to end up like this guy?"

I was obsessed with the taste of it.

My father picked me up and sat me up on his shoulders to go out as promised.

"But there is food at home!" my mother said, accusing him of spoiling me.

"Darling, let me do what he asks me for, at least on the weekends." he told her with a kiss.

"Well, grab me one with you then," my mother answered with a smile.

We drove to a close-by shawarma spot next to our house. I ate my tiny little sandwich and then we headed back home so he can sit with mom for some time. I was utterly the happiest kid on earth.

There was once a void I was living in, a place where everything seemed so smooth, problem-free, under the wings of my father, I wasn't afraid of anything. I can't recall any memories of worrying or even thinking about my stuttering. It was a time when I didn't even know I had a problem.

It all started to get clear in my first grade of school with my first ever experience with stuttering when my teacher asked me to read an English paragraph in class as me and my classmates took turns.

"Khaled, page twenty-five, the second paragraph please," the teacher said,

"PPPPaul wakes up every MMMorning and GGGoes to school BBy bus."

I continued the paragraph with not much stuttering at that time. While there was silence in the class during my reading, I could still hear some kids who were trying to hold their laughs every time I read.

Reading out loud in the classroom got me introduced to my stutter; it rather opened my eyes that I am not like other kids, that I am different.

I went home from school with so many questions.

Why am I speaking like this?

Why am I not like the others?

Why are they reacting like that when I read?

I didn't even know what's stuttering at that time; just like all the other kids, as a boy, my innocuous interests were to play, eat, and see my friends, shooting at bad people with my favorite wooden pistol.

The next day, I had another reading class. Sitting at the third desk from the left row, usually copying what the teacher is writing on the board until the teacher said.

"It's reading time!"

We started reading one paragraph at a time, each kid. I was experiencing a new behavior; it was the first time I felt and got introduced to the word "panic" not knowing what to expect from my reading; I was sweating, my heartbeats increasing every time my turn gets closer.

What's going on with my body?

I don't want my turn to come, I even want to go out of the classroom, but I can't.

I want to go home and play with my father.

All of that was going inside my mind while the turns are moving.

My turn came in a blink of an eye; my throat was already dry; I swallowed and started to read.

"ShShShShShe wwwwwent to ppppplay with her bbbbbrother and hhhhis friends *out of breath* iiiin the ppppark."

It was my second speech in front of the class that year. I continued the paragraph; surprisingly, I was stuttering even worse than the first time, clueless of the reason why at that time. A dozen of my classmates had read in class, all told without stuttering. But as soon as I tried to read one more time, the words just wouldn't come out of my mouth correctly. I tried to slow down, but that just made me sound worse. When the ordeal was over, I slunk back to my seat.

"Good job, Khaled! Kids, everyone applauds!" Mrs. Jenny told me. But it was all too obvious it was a lie.

The teacher decided to order the classroom to applaud me as a kind of encouragement, and she have been doing it since then. She thought that she was helping when in fact she wasn't. This only left me with more questions. If only she understood that she was making things worse.

Why me?

Why are they applauding only for me?

I knew then that I am different.

Days passed by in school, by time, in reading classes, when my turn came, I didn't read a whole paragraph like other students. The teacher thought I didn't notice that she reduced my reading phrases as not to waste the time of the class; on the other hand, I was so gifted as a child I used to notice everything silently.

By the end of the year, I used to read a phrase or a couple of lines every English reading class, followed by "A round of applause."

I am seven years old; Nour was born, a little angel who shed light on the whole family. I had a lovely sister, I cared for her, fed her, played with her, and most importantly, I always brushed her hair. My parents were surprised about the way I treat her, especially that my other two brothers were not acting the same way.

She was undeniably my first love. As she grew up, her hair got thicker, longer, and more mesmerizing, making it harder for me to brush.

"Mommy, I don't want Khaled to brush my hair, come please." She kept refusing as she wanted her mother to do it, but I learned the right way and was doing it even better than mom by time.

She started developing a character of her own, a strong and compelling one; she was a lioness as a horoscope, she used to stand for my little brother in school if he's facing some troubles with someone, boys used to avoid her. She was so fierce yet so beautiful and innocent for a little girl. When she came back from school every day, I fed her, helped her do her homework, and sang her bedtime lullabies.

She made me forget about my stutter for some time; I was occupied with something else, loving someone else, emotionally connected, and not focused on the disability I had.

My parents used to care about sports; I had to practice various sports as a kid, starting from swimming, gymnastics, football, basketball, karate, and even shooting. They wanted to see me shine in one sport, so I could pursue my path in it; they always wanted the best for me and my brothers as athletes.

Surprisingly enough, I used to shine in every sport I step foot in, I was the star in swimming classes where my coach used to speak with my parents about my future as an athlete swimmer, a perfect gymnast who is ready to enter competitions at a young age and a talented basketball team player where they asked my parents to add me to the roster of the club team of the city we lived in, I didn't know back then how my future life as an athlete will be, but it looked promising.

Unfortunately, I didn't make use of all of that at that age.

My family used to be constantly leaving the country on mid-year and final year school vacations to visit my home country, for a period of three months annually, and so normally, it affected my life as an athlete, not a single coach or trainer agreed on such level of commitment.

Back to school, troubles started to unwind in the third grade when bullying started to make its way upon me, a classmate who obviously didn't like the way I talk.

Amr was the bully. A dark eyed tall boy who was too muscular for his age, he had a loud and resonating laugh and he was known for his scar over his left eye-brow.

He towered over the first years and took their lunch money. He teased the fat kids and anyone he suspected of being gay. He didn't care if they were or not, just so long as his crew laughed. They weren't really his friends, he thought of them as mates, but if he ever had a problem, these were not the people to bare your soul to. They hung with him because they enjoyed the thrill of power. And to be honest, he liked it too. It gave him a feeling of security he couldn't get another way. Whenever he was abused at home, or the teachers gave him another failing grade, he could just shut down, lock it out. He was someone who commanded respect, and only a fool would mess with him.

When the school bell rang for break time, he used to come to tease me on purpose.

"Hey, Khaled, what are you going to say to me today."

"NNNNothing, do yyyyou have a ppproblem?"

"M-M-My p-p-problem i-i-is y-y-you." He laughed sarcastically in the school corridor.

Every time he used to approach me, I used to wait for that inner voice of mine to tell me something, but it has been mute for quite a long time.

By time he threw a nickname on me, which was then repeated by a few kids in school walking in the bully's shadow. I was called "The crippled."

Just by the time I decided to stand up for myself, I carried my backpack at the end of the school day, tied my shoes, and started walking slowly toward the bully, having a thousand words lurking in my head to say to him. Something inside me was telling me not to go.

It's that voice again, but it had a different tone, a more fragile one; it was powerless, not the one I was used to.

On a try to ignore it, I went to the bully.

"You are a pig." I cursed him in public.

That day, I got myself into a fight where I got beaten. Although I had some body bruises, the mental bruises were much deeper, which made me think; maybe I should've listened to that voice.

"Am I on my own?" I asked myself, I asked him.

I didn't get an answer

I then realized that my inner voice and best friend are gone and will not come back, ever.

I lost all the confidence I once had, I was helplessly looking for someone to tell me that I am strong enough to stand up for myself and teach that bully a lesson, but no one ever helped.

Time passed, my father was noticing my stutter; he was always busy and didn't give my stutter the full attention it needed to have; he wasn't able to understand what's going on with me, always thought that I am making it all up.

One day, he told me, "Khaled, you got to speak like other kids," he said.

A phrase that always kept on ringing in my head, I often asked myself.

"But how?"

How, when I don't even know how to tame it?

And so, I laid my head on the bed and woke up to another day.

I am eleven years old, it's three weeks until my birthday, and all I think about is this one gift I want the most to ask my father to get me.

It was a hot April's weekend; The sunlight beams through my bedroom, infiltrates that same window where it all started, its rays warming up my bed, my brothers are still sleeping, I woke up and wiped my eyes with the back of my hands, I went to wash my face and then to the living room, there was a letter on the table.

"Sweethearts, I, Dad, and Nour went to Dubai to do some shopping; we will be back soon; here is some money for you and your brothers to order some food until we come. See you soon.

Love. Mom."

I jumped happily, took the letter, picked up the money, and handed them to my bigger brother.

"We will eat shawarma today!" I said to him.

"All you think about is shawarma." He mocked me.

In a few hours, the food was ordered, served, and eaten. We kept playing the whole day long; I invited my best friend who lived next door to play some final fantasy on my PlayStation; the day passed so fast, my friend went home back to his family, while I was still waiting for mine to come back.

27

The streets were getting darker, and the moon lights started to enter our home through the windows; I went to stand in our fourth-floor balcony, gazing on the streets waiting for my mother, father, and sister to come home, the noise of the big city was getting calmer, and the lights in the windows of the neighboring buildings were getting turned off, one after the other. We kept calling them on their phones that night, but they never answered.

It was my first night to sleep without my parents, without kissing father good night, and without reading Nour her bedtime story; I closed my eyes and forced myself to sleep.

When I Woke up the next day, I rushed to my parent's room; their bed was the same as I left it, mom's makeup cosmetics still in the same order as she left it, and their bathroom door was still closed.

Their room was empty; our home was cold and creepy. We managed to keep ourselves busy that day, playing with our neighbors and friends, but something didn't smell right.

I took my younger brother between my arms as he was starting to cry; we slept for another night alone, one more day in a deserted house.

It's the third day already; my younger brother was crying hysterically; I was so young to take responsibility for him, and so was my elder brother, who was only fourteen at the time; we were young, not even knowing who to call and what to do.

I was asking my elder brother questions, a lot of questions where he himself was standing clueless for it.

Karim, my elder brother, stepped up at that time, where he had a suggestion to call all the hospitals in the region;

while I managed to calm down my little brother, Karim, and I had a feeling that something's not right, we just didn't know what it was.

In my parent's room, there was a phone that my dad always used for work. Karim took out a paper with a list of hospitals and started calling every single one of them; every hospital my brother called confirmed they know nothing about the aforementioned people.

"Maybe we should call the police?" I told my elder brother.

"No, not now," he answered.

Until we came to the last hospital on the list, he dialed the number; Karim is on the line, while I am standing right in front of him, listening to the following conversation.

"Hello, who's this?"

"Hello, my name is Karim Bassyouny, and I am looking for my family; I was wondering if you have any patients with these names (he listed the full names of my mother, my father, and Nour)."

(Silence)

"And who would you be?"

"I am the elder son of the family. Do you know anything about the aforementioned people?"

"How old are you?"

"Fourteen."

"Is there anyone older I can speak to?"

"No, there is no one, and I am old enough; what's wrong?"

(Silence)

"Hello?"

"There was a family who arrived two days ago, following a tragic road accident on the highway to Dubai, a family consisting of a father of forty-three years, a mother of thirty-nine, and a five-year-old small girl.

Sadly we couldn't save the life of the girl; the father was reported dead on the spot of the accident, while the girl died between the hands of the nurse on the way while rushing to the operation room following severe cranial trauma. The mother is currently vitally stable in the intensive care unit but has suffered multiple fractures all over the body and hemi paralysis of the face.

We were looking for any member of their family, but we couldn't recognize any coordinates as the car was totally damaged and we weren't able to retrieve anything from it, the car was chain sawed, and the bodies were taken to the hospital by a helicopter.

Hello, are you still there?"

(Silence)

Chapter 3
The Sail

Death wasn't kind. It snatched where it could, taking people who were far too young, far too good. It didn't pretend to care; it didn't pretend to distinguish.

They say not to mourn the passing of a life well-lived, yet celebrate. That we should count the times, our souls smiled together, reached out so invisibly yet tangibly and touched. But I was so young to understand. Young to understand that death is only the end of a chapter, and the beginning of another.

And so, Karim hung up the phone without saying a word.

That look on his face couldn't be overlooked and will always be remembered; his face was red, his body was sweaty, and his eyes just about to burst into tears.

"Father and Nour died." He told me while holding his tears.

"Where is mom?" I said.

"She's in the hospital; she's okay."

What is Death? What does that even mean? Aren't they coming back? Will I not see them again?

I had many uncertainties as a kid for the news I just heard; I remember I didn't shed a single tear, I was emotionless; matter of fact, I was so confused to the extent that I wasn't aware of what does this news really mean and what are the consequences.

My younger brother woke up; I left Karim in the room where he continued to make additional calls starting with my uncle, who lived not far away from our home; I went to check on my younger brother, hugged him, and put him back to sleep.

In a blink of an eye, our home was full of people, relatives, and friends, some hugging me, some crying, some giving me food and chocolates which I didn't ask for, and some were just sitting there staring at our family pictures hanging on the walls.

Among this crowd, there was my mother's best friend and wife of my father's business partner and much like a brother, their family having three boys and a girl just like us; they used to always visit us and their kids used to hang out at our home regularly, they were like family members.

They were the first ones standing by us in these difficult times, not knowing back then that their father is going to be our lifetime court opponent and that our friendship will turn to enmity.

I called my best friend, who was living two blocks away from me at that time, and narrated to him what's going on.

"Khaled, stop joking around, see you at school," he said, laughing and hung up.

We didn't sleep alone that night.

School was never missed; my uncle made sure we continue our academic year without any distractions. Every

32

day I would come home, I would see many people in our cozy living room supporting us, many kids, and many faces.

But her face was never one of them.

I was missing her.

The incident went viral and in a couple of days it was all over the local newspaper; they even took a day off at my sister's school as a tribute to her loss.

My uncle took Karim and went on a visit to the hospital to check on my mother and finish the paperwork that was needed for the transportation of the corpses of my father and my sister Nour back to my home country to get buried there and make a proper funeral. Karim got to see their faces one more time before they get transported, but I didn't.

To this day, it's the only thing I envy my brother about.

I wonder why my uncle didn't take me too, and what he was thinking, giving this opportunity only to my elder brother.

One last look to Nour's round face and beautiful wide eyes. One last glance to my father's beard and forehead wrinkles. I was craving it. But I didn't get the chance to lay eyes on them one last time.

My mother was healing, slowly and steady, but progressive.

All the previous years, my relation with my mother was so shallow, not knowing anything about her personal life, didn't know her age, interests, even her full name; for me, she was just "Mom."

Until she stepped up in my life at that time when she returned home, she got discharged from the hospital and stepped her first steps back in her house two weeks after the

33

accident, this time without the love of her life and her only long-awaited daughter.

I ran to her and hugged her; she wasn't able to hug me back as strong as before; she was still healing, her fractures were fresh, her body was drained, and there was a big scar next to her right ear.

I remember her face as if I saw her yesterday; her eyes were weak, full of tears, full of questions, queries about the future of her life and her kids.

How will she continue?

Who will take care of our expenses?

Will she have to find a job as soon as possible?

What will she do with her love life?

A broken-hearted widow at a young age, she was.

The crowds in our home started to diminish, day by day, until we gradually returned to our normal life, but with a family of four, a single mother, and three little boys.

It was too much for my mother to continue in the same city, same home, everything there reminded her of her previous life, and she needed the support of her family as well.

The school year came to an end, and we found ourselves packing to leave the country where my father used to work, saying farewell to everything beautiful I had, all my childhood friends, and the streets where I had built all of my memories. We returned back to start a new life, this time only the four of us. We returned back to my home country, Egypt.

Now you're probably wondering what did I do with my stutter. Well, it got worse as I finally got introduced to Taurus.

Chapter 4
Taurus

Your only easy day was yesterday.

A phrase that keeps running through my head over and over.

So here I come, the big city, Land of the pharaohs, as they would say, only for me it didn't smell like pharaohs at all, but rather frustration and worrying about how I will cope with the community, having not lived there for the previous twelve years of my life.

As a city kid, I still need what my ancestors did; I need what humans evolved to need. In these concrete streets, I need trees, birdsong, flowers. I need fresh air, good food, and a chance to play with friends freely, feeling safe and loved. We, like other animals, can't adapt so quickly to large changes.

My father working abroad for quite a long time had got us financially covered for years and years ahead; he invested his savings in an apartment back in Cairo, a home he was planning to come back and relocate in with his wife and four kids, he had a plan, however, sometimes God has a whole different plan.

My mother spent a couple of months searching for good schools to register us in; she finally chose a school not far from our new home.

It was the first day in my new school, with different faces than those I used to see; the kids did speak the same language I spoke but with a totally different dialect than the one I knew, gave me some hard time understanding them.

The clock ticked thirteen zero zero when there was an orientation gathering for all the classes of my same grade; it was a pretty big school, much bigger than the one I was in, a number of almost seventy students gathered in a big hall, along with all the teachers for different subjects.

It's the introduction time; everyone gets to introduce himself, his full name, age, and his favorite hobby.

A good first impression was all I wished for at that time.

The game of turns commenced, and so did the game of panic.

"Pfft, you're gonna mess up big time."

I turned around to see if someone was speaking to me.

But no one was there.

"Can you imagine all of these people will burst into laughter when they hear you speak?"

This must not be real; who's this, where is this voice coming from, and what does it want from me.

Tick-Tock "Khaled, your turn, could you introduce yourself to your friends and classmates please."

(Silence)

All eyes were upon me; I stood up, I decided to give it a shot, it's just a name, an age, and a damn hobby, after all, isn't it.

I remember it was the longest time I have ever said my name; I started noticing some new movements happening to my body, more like jerks as I am forcing the words out, facial muscle twitches, it's interesting how the human body reacts to different situations, however, even with the jerks accompanying the speech, the words didn't get out anyway, so it not only made me stutter but also made me look like a psychopath.

I managed to finish my one-minute introduction in almost five. Five minutes of sweating, palpitations, twitches and forcing the words out. And in case you're curious, yes, they laughed; everyone did, including the teachers.

The school day was over; I went home, I cried solely, as much as I know that my mother loved me, I didn't want to bother her with my problems, to add my load to hers, as for almost for the first year since we moved back to Egypt, I used to enter her room and see her weeping alone, the burden was heavy, I didn't want to make it heavier, the effect of the accident on her psychologically was still not getting any better.

I preferred to deal with my own issues solo; for the time being, a matter of fact, all I ever needed was to come back home and play with Nour again like I used to.

But wait, that voice, is it really there again?

That day was my first time I actually sob due to my stutter; admitting that I have a disability wasn't an easy thing, a disability that's interrupting my day-to-day life, and apparently will continue doing that until further notice.

How come I didn't cry when I lost my father, but I am shedding tears on this exact incident? I know why, because it was hurtful, I did care much about giving the perfect first impression. Nevertheless, no matter what first impact I wanted to make, a lesson was learned that day.

It is not to ever expect a good first impression if you stutter; stop giving it that much attention. And give yourself some time to fix it later.

In my case, I didn't fix anything; I didn't even try; I rather started isolating myself from my classmates, ate my lunch alone; it was that age where young boys usually start every bad habit possibly possible, skipping classes, hiding to get a smoke and exchanging pictures of nude girls for fun.

I, however, was so detached that I didn't even know these things existed at such age. I was also raised in a family, choosing for me whom I should be friends with and with whom I should not; I was told not to be friends with bad boys; for me, I did it, not because I wanted to, but because it wasn't even a choice, I wouldn't dream of being friends with these boys, not knowing at that time that one day, I'll be that boy who people would dream to make friends with.

Two years have passed, and my stutter wasn't progressing a single bit.

My mother, on the other hand, was improving physically, mentally, and psychologically.

It took her a while, but she finally started slowly to regain back her life; she stood back on her feet, she started looking for a job to maintain our living costs, wanting to provide us with everything we need, she was the mother, the father, and the sister at the same time, she had a dream to raise three big boys to be proud of one day, with many sacrifices done from her side, she refused to marry another man, she devoted herself, her life and all her time to us and to me, she developed into a hero in my eyes.

She started to notice what stuttering is doing to my life and where it is driving me; while watching in agony, never knowing where to start and what to do, she started taking me to doctors, various type of doctors, speech therapists, hypnotherapists, she was even told that it was some kind of a curse or magic cast upon me that's holding my tongue, where we made numerous visits to specialists in that field too, we also tried "Hijama" an old traditional Arabic religious therapy method, which is known today as 'wet cupping' or 'cupping therapy' medicine where blood is drawn by vacuum from a small skin incision for therapeutic purposes. Now becoming popular among many sportsmen, however, did any of this help?

Well, while with the speech therapists, the approach to my stutter at that time was that old lame approach, the "take a breath and speak slowly" method, not to mention that nowadays the speech therapists are more knowledgeable with more exposure to stuttering accompanied by different methods and approaches to it, despite their failure of all their methods on me, something really strange was happening to me at that time, I used to speak flawlessly while in the sessions, with minimal or almost no stutter, they've put me to read books, newspaper, and even poems.

The stutter just disappeared.

"Your son is treated as you can see."

They used to say to my mother after I finish my sessions. This being said and surely followed by mom believing that it's over as she was there during the sessions.

Nevertheless, as soon as I got back to my ordinary life, the stutter found its way back just as easy.

Time after time, it changed to a routine; I go to the therapist, I would play their game, speaking in their turtle talk method, easy on-sets unnatural but fluent way while I am there, and even while being in my mother's car driving back home after being told I am doing great, however when we would get back home, I would talk in my normal voice and not that strangers voice, at home and in school, until the next trip.

Session after session, for many days, months, years, money was spent, time and effort, just to attain fluency, but it's stuck there; it didn't want to part. I have always had that feeling that this thing, this disability, is much deeper than that; it's deeper than going to a speaking session, taking a breath and murmuring some words or whatever is written, its more about how you look at it, your view from up there, how big or how small you see it.

Not any other method was effective.

Four years later, I finished secondary school; by the end of this period of my life, I have got myself a whole set of complexes in my character that needs to be taken care of or perhaps to be treated; socializing was a no-no for me, any situation I was put in I would immediately develop a panic, let alone seeing or talking with a girl, which was a nightmare.

That voice in my head was following me in every panic situation; it reminded me of the voice I always heard as a child, pushing me to be my very best, but that voice felt different; it wasn't pushing me forward, giving me the confidence I urge, but perhaps, robbing it from me, eating me alive.

I redeveloped the habit of speaking with it again when we're alone; sometimes, I was caught by people around me asking me who am I speaking with.

There were nights where I used to remember my old friend and compare him to these voices in my head now.

I got myself literally three friends out of these four years of school; we used to hang out on the weekends; I'll always remember this time we went to a famous fast-food restaurant to grab something to eat.

It was when I was looking at the menu, wondering what to order for myself until I chose a meal starting with the letter "B" one of my worse letters; a Barbeque Chicken Burger.

"You better choose something else," he said.

"But why, I want to have that," I whispered to myself.

"Unless you want to spend the next five minutes stuttering while ordering your food, embarrassing yourself and the line you're standing in, you should listen to me and order this hotdog."

"But…"

"Your order, sir?" asked the young girl on the cashier.

"Hotdog, please," I answered.

I became more aware of the habits I relied on to communicate, like substituting words, which sometimes even left with an incomplete thought, not focusing on people's facial expressions, adding filler words like "umm" and "eh," all of these fears and compensations led to a lack of confidence and a terrifying fear of speaking in public, even ordering my own food was a struggle that it became a habit to order the food that's easier to say rather than what I really want.

Until I came home that night after I ate the hotdog, I entered my room and locked the door, and I asked him the questions I longed to have their answers.

"Who are you? What made you change, and why are you doing this?"

"I am Taurus, or would you prefer 'The Crippled'? Maybe I changed, but it's all your guilt, you made me that way, and I won't let you humiliate me more; I will listen to your worst fears. I will understand what makes you tick. Then I'll control you like a remotely controlled toy. I'll start you out with small tasks you find distasteful and work you up to things you never dreamed you were capable of.

I'll dangle the illusion of confidence before you and let you get close enough to almost attain it. Then I'll just ask you for one more little thing, to prove your devotion, of course. When you have become the person your old self would have loathed beyond all others, I will disappear. Why? Because that is the end of my game, and you mean nothing to me. You can call me your worst nightmare; if you stutter, you should hide from the eyes of the people and don't put me in these situations anymore, I would, and I will stand in front of you in everything you want to achieve just to protect you."

Unless he was mistaken, he didn't want to protect me.

I got that answer right away; it was harsh, it was creepy, his voice was shaky yet so determined to do what he promised, it was another side of me, an evil side of my zodiac self, it was the voice of Taurus.

Since then and over the years, when speaking with him, I did never stutter, I didn't like what he had become, I was always trying to stand against him, in constant attempts of proving him wrong and not letting him control me. Unfortunately, I would fail, over and over.

While having many thoughts and words in my head and not being able to set them free, I always had that urge to say everything I want to say without the feeling that someone is looking at what I am saying or how am I saying it.

I came back from school one day, I found my mother cleaning up some sealed boxes related to my father's old work documents and Nour's school copybooks from her previous French school, something drew me to a copybook of hers, I grabbed it in my hands, blew away the dust off its cover and I found myself turning the first page of it just to find a kids' poem she took in class at the time.

That song, this melody, I remember she always came back home and sang it for me and innocently clapping for her own self right after, which usually made me laugh. It's still resounding in my head; it was written by her own hands.

I took the copybook, later that night, I started writing my feelings in it; on that exact date and almost five years after the accident, I started writing the first page of my own daily diaries in her school copybook, and since then, opening my diaries always made me feel her presence.

Despite all of the stutter I had, I was an exceptional student; I had good grades in school due to my social isolation, more like a nerd with no friends. However, I didn't stay like that for long; my academic grades took the downhill plunge as I got attached to a new habit, a thing that clinched me and took me to a different world by the age of sixteen as I slid into the path of addiction.

Chapter 5
Shyva

For many, addiction comes in only one face, the alcoholic who drinks himself to death or the drug addict who overdoses on crack cocaine, but is it really sicker than a kid who spends twenty hours daily in front of a computer screen?

When the pain comes, my brain makes a million excuses to cave in, and I only need one. My thoughts are as a brilliant rat in a very bad maze, for it's just too easy to solve. Then I'm there, at my addiction, awaiting a new fix, praying I can survive this "cure" for the never-ending search for comfort.

It was a feeling that was long missed more like a euphoria. I finally found the social life I've been dreaming of, without the need to speak.

By virtue of a friend of mine, we used to often frequent a computer gaming club near my home, disengage from the world, and play together the video games we like.

Video games affect the brain in the same way as addictive drugs, as they trigger the release of dopamine; I "needed" to play video games to be happy and felt extremely miserable when am not playing, conveying a disorder that is just as real as alcoholism or dependence on prescription drugs. It is what now to be diagnosed by the World Health Organization as "internet gaming disorder."

My life deteriorated. I neglected everything and everyone around me. I abandoned my other hobbies. I lost sleep. And my social life evaporated.

I know it's an addiction. Everyone told me. But it's too painful to let go of. It's always there for me when nothing else is. It makes my brain feel happy again. And I feel so bad to just let go.

Online gaming was my own sort of drug and my everlasting getaway.

It was the year of releasing one of the best online gaming platforms in the world which is probably running until now. I got my own character, my own persona behind a black screen, everyone respected me based on what I type, with no chains attached, I was saying anything to anyone I want with nil panic indicator; it was a stutter-free world. We were all the same; I just didn't feel different there. I built the virtual social life I wanted, and most importantly, I always left good first impressions there.

While in my first year of university, I almost had zero social skills; I was afraid of people, girls were not even on my map, unlike my elder brother at that time, I used to always watch him surrounded by girls and grabbing phone numbers just as easy. He mingled well with the opposite sex; at some point, I had some jealousy lurking inside of me; he was living the life I was dreaming of living myself.

One day, I was walking on our school campus when a girl approached me.

"Heyyy, are you Maha's relative?" she asked with a cute smile.

"Yes," I answered facing the ground.

"I am Sarah, her very close friend; you can call me Sue!"

"SSSorry I don't remember you," I answered, and I left.

It's more like I escaped; I left her standing by herself while we were in the middle of a conversation; I didn't say anything. No "I have to go," no "I'll catch you later," not even "bye." I just left.

I was turning to a creature who gets anxious when a shadow of a stranger gets close to him, and the more I have failures of not expressing myself with random people, the more I get more drawn to my gaming life.

As a teenager, I wouldn't say I was an angel, but I wasn't that troublesome either, the maximum that I could do is to tell lies, like telling my mother I was at school when I wasn't, always believed that I could've been worse with a lot more bad tendencies, but isolation and mainly my stutter didn't let me.

And so, I failed my first two years of university without even acknowledging it; I was in a different world, someone else's planet, the world of a girl called Shyva, my game character, in a realm full of friends, fun, killing monsters, riding mounts and raiding instances, following my high level of dedication to the game I became one of the top-ranked players worldwide that I was chosen to try the game's beta version before even launching. Unquestionably, what do you expect of someone who wakes up to sit on his computer for around twenty hours straight, give or take.

New friends were made in the gaming cafe I used to go to and skip university, some of them are still my friends until now, some I lost contact with, we hanged together online all day and at intervals, all night as well when there were holidays.

I used to go out in the morning, take my backpack with some books in it, pretend as if am going to my classes, and come home the time my classes finish so my mother would think that I was at the university; I developed my first bad habit, I was a liar.

Although I had a few unpleasant moments regarding my stuttering as well with the new friends I made back in that gaming club, but I loved the place so much that I didn't want to leave.

The voice in my head, Taurus, on the contrary, was mute as long as I am in my comfort zone; I didn't want to face it, my real villain, I didn't want to confront him just now, but there, I faced a lot of villains, online, I wiped them all out, there, I didn't feel different, I felt free.

But before I tell you how I got out of this pit, let me tell you what was happening to a mother witnessing all of this happening to her child, not being like other kids, neither enjoying his life as a teenager, a game addict, a young man who has absolutely no clear future after failing two years in a row in the university which subsequently created a lot of tension between us in that period.

My mother finally got a job, I used to not see her as I used to, after attempting too many methods and treatments to my stutter, she was standing helpless in front of it, but she always believed I should someday gain my fluent speech back, she was knocking all the doors, after all, a door should open, shouldn't it.

Sadly, all the doors knocked, and all approaches that were made were on the wrong track.

She was missing the most important door.

To give me the confidence I was hungry for.

But I wasn't her only obstacle; disputes started to arise with my father's business partner and friend when he said to my grandfather:

"Sorry your son died, but you have nothing in this company now, neither his kids."

My grandfather was always after our rights; he wanted to secure our share in the heritage before his time comes as his three helpless grandsons in the share of my father's company.

My father's partner refused to give us our share, claiming that my father didn't own anything with him; I used to see my mother wake up every morning, meeting with my grandfather and our lawyer to travel to Alexandria for the court, a case that took more than a decade to end, she never lost hope neither did she get bored, she stood for our rights until the last day.

That wasn't her only problem, parallelly she had to deal with my elder brother who started doing drugs as a teenager, my younger brother who had bowel diseases that needed to be constantly operated on, or even me, an isolated non-social creature who also happens to be an addict.

After knocking on enough doors for a cure, a day came where I finally told my mother that I want to go to another school, a school for the deaf; I explained to her that I would prefer to be categorized and treated as deaf than to go out to the world every day and face what am facing, at least there I will have to deal with people like me, and I won't feel any different. As much as this hurt her but she never showed. She always told me I have nothing major and that one day it will go away.

By sixteen, writing my diaries became a habit, never knowing at that time that someday I would tell a story out of it. My main purpose was to write my true feelings, those feelings that no one would ever know due to my stutter; speaking to myself and soothing myself was my breakout in one way or the other; I used to write how did my day go, my impressions on different people, things I wanted to say but I couldn't, I was even answering my villain there, telling him how much I hate him.

Although I almost never looked back on what I wrote. It was like letting go a bird out of a cage, or perhaps letting go the words from my heart, it was then when I learned that *one of the hardest things in life is having words in your heart that you can't utter.*

Days passed by, my mother decided to take us on a family vacation just like my father used to do; every one of us, me and my brothers, had his own issues and problems in life, she decided that every one of us needs a break and that we need to spend some quality time all together.

While on vacation, on a sunny day, on the dazzling shores of the Mediterranean Sea and after screwing my first two years of university, I was sitting with my mother in a moment of tranquility, while she was randomly browsing the newspaper, she came across an advertisement for studying abroad, a country I knew just a little about, she showed me the ad and said:

"Khaled, I think it's time you take a little responsibility for yourself. Are you interested in studying abroad in the field you've been dreaming of?"

She asked me curiously.

With the tension between me and my mother reaching its peak at that time, I was quite excited to go; I don't remember I was hesitant or uncertain; in fact, all I looked at that time was that I'd be able to play my games in peace without that constant pressure from her about my future, eating all that junk food I desire all day, and maybe losing more years of studying facing that black screen. Those were merely the things on my mind at that time.

A few weeks later, I found myself packing for a life-changing journey, a teenager, all alone, starting my first day in medical university.

The airplane felt like home; I could curl up and sleep as easily as dozing on the couch. The engines roared and the winded buffeted; it was like my sky-born cradle, rocked by the winds far above the ground. Even as the engines turned, my brain relaxed into dreaming mode, there were thousands of miles to go, and all I had to do was let this technological bird fly me there, fly me to the beautiful lands of Ukraine.

Chapter 6
Metamorphosis

I am Eighteen.

Green city, fresh air and beautiful girls.

Having mixed feelings, the joy of being all alone with no one to control my actions and nagging me about my gaming life, I can finally spend all the time I want on my computer, but at the same time, I have this feeling of concern as soon as I left my family, I sure am not used to living alone, being 'mommas boy' for so long got me accustomed to not worrying about the household, cooking, paying my bills, and much more things that were set on auto for me, I was scared to face all of this alone without my mother, my brothers and my friends, after all, I didn't move to another street or district, it's a whole new country, with different people and mentalities, different language and a totally new culture I knew nothing about. I wanted to be accepted; I wanted to change, I had a goal but was it ever taken seriously?

I spent the first couple of weeks on trials to change, exerting a little bit more effort on socializing and trying a little bit harder to know new people and widen my circle of colleagues; I was trying to break out to the real world.

I suddenly got more interested to know more about stuttering, researching it in all aspects, what is it really about? And how can it "go away."

I spent some time surfing the internet for countries that have somehow found a miraculous cure for it, I was for some reason convinced that somewhere in someplace in the world they've found something that could make it disappear, I was so naive to believe it's true.

I came across an online forum for stutterers where they share their life stories regarding stuttering, they shared it as a kind of support; as soon as I entered that forum, it was like a portal to a new world, a world full of people just like me, they supported each other.

There was a time where I thought I was the only one in this world who was going through such life scenes that no one would ever be going through what I am going through; I thought that no one would relate.

I am glad I was wrong.

I remember the first time I read about a cure through means of hypnotherapy; I laughed hysterically, not because I didn't believe it's real, neither was I making fun of it, somewhat, I was laughing by amusement and joy, just the idea that there is a mere one percent probability out there of getting me cured when I thought there was no hope was enough to boost my mood for days and days.

I used to spend hours and hours reading every stutterer's adventures, just to relate with mine, it would make me feel better, at least for a little time.

I got my first phone call from abroad; it was my mother, she was crying, telling me how much she misses me, she used to tell me how I left a big space in our home since I left, her love was real. However, I was so young to understand that I didn't feel the same way, a typical teenager I was.

Living in the campus dorms, which were full of students my same age, boys and girls, I remember there I met the first girl with whom I actually had a normal conversation. I was that typical "Mr. Nice Guy" type of guy. Trying hard to satisfy everyone and worrying so much about how and what they think about me, which got me abused in many different ways later on.

Interestingly enough, I met new people in my life that had different reactions to my stuttering; it was always amazing to see how random people react to it, moreover, I seemed to enjoy classifying them and putting them into different genres; it was my own little game, it was fun.

So some people used to laugh, thinking that I am a perfect comedian and that I am making it all up; I called them "the easy-going," some used to stay away from me thinking that I am a freak, whom I called "the phobic," some looked at me not knowing what's going on and clueless on how to react, these people are "the shocked" type, some just avoided eye contact with me these are "the embarrassed," some offered me help by continuing my sentence "the helpers" you'll meet them a lot these days, and some people started giving me "real precious" advice on how to speak fluently by narrating how their so and so relatives got treated by doing this and that, it's always a pleasure meeting the "Mr. Know it all" type of people. However, the worst reaction of all is the sympathy reaction, or so I call it, where they start to pity you. That reaction always got me in the feels.

Whenever I faced a bad experience in the real world regarding my stutter, I knew that I've always had a rebound; I was waiting to get back home and log into my online world again, return to my cocoon again, just to feel better.

Lacking the will to persevere in the real world, it wasn't long until I bounced back to my comfort zone, connected my laptop, and logged online. My whole world was revolving around Shyva, as if I didn't want to get out of my bubble, so scared to get hurt again and breaking out those chains just seemed so far and unattainable.

I spent my whole first year of university in my dorm room; somehow, I managed to never miss my classes and maintain my home studies as well; I was studying the thing I love, medicine.

I passed my first year of medical school while seeing students my age spending their days hanging out, drinking, and partying while my days were all about classes, online gaming, studying. I didn't even get to speak with my classmates; I kept on intending to isolate myself.

Flying back to Egypt on vacation to visit my family, my mother, who was so proud of the success I achieved as I passed my first year in medical school, and so was I.

But my first journey back home was an eye-opener on a lot of matters that I had to get fixed in my life.

I started witnessing my mother's aging; she's still running in the courts to retrieve our rights in heritage from my father's business partner, but she was alone this time; my grandfather had passed away while I was abroad, he breathed his last words to my mother.

"Don't give up on the kid's share of their father's company; continue your path."

I saw Karim carrying all the burden of the family by himself as the bigger brother, and I saw my younger brother just starting his teenage life.

Going back to Ukraine for my second year of medical school, I had one thing in mind, I knew I have to decrease my online playing time gradually. With the intention to pay more focus to the stuff that is imperative in this period.

However, I didn't know how and where to start; I couldn't even imagine staying one day without logging online.

But it happened; I irrevocably curbed the addiction in my second year of medical school, but not the way I wanted it to end, as my computer ceased to function, in addition to facing difficulties paying my monthly game subscriptions.

I involuntarily lived with these conditions for a whole year; it was like I was forced to quit, compelled to get exposed to the real world; I felt like I was handcuffed, held by the face, imposed to open my eyes in front of a very bright light.

I spent six months in hell; it was the withdrawal effects of five years of hardcore gaming, I mean, all I wanted was to take it one step at a time, cutting it abruptly made a sudden void in my every day, there was a huge gap of time I didn't know where and how to employ it.

I started to have dreams of my game character and my online virtual so-called friends, but worse of all, I had nightmares of my previous stuttering experiences as if they recall back, and the voices in my head started to appear once again.

Taurus came back as I started to get more involved in daily conversations, but this time more fierce and aggressive.

Taurus was like a trapped soul, too scared to move on, desperate not to stay. He had accumulated so much guilt throughout the years, over and over. He started roaming as a spirit in my moments of loneliness and emptiness; to him, I was like a haunted house, over time, the loneliness took over from the relief of solitude, and he came to the opinion that it was God who is the reason for all of that. He became angry; his energy warped until there was none left, not destroyed but mutated into something so vile that he could never be saved. Not content to haunt or even be a poltergeist, he learned how to whisper in my ears. He learned how to appear so that only I could see him and feel his presence. Once a best friend, he became the self-styled enemy of myself. The natural order to him was fear, greed, and power. When he was tired of his petty malice, he came to me to control, not as a possession, but to whisper evil actions to me and watch while I carried them out.

And so, for the first time, I finally started looking at people's faces in the university, giving attention to learning a new language and practicing it. Of course, with a stutter, it was even worse; I started regularly attending my lectures which I used to pass on when I was gaming, I hardly made new friends.

I started to realize that I have a crush on a girl in the same year as I am, I had a strong desire to just go and open up a conversation with her, but I was so mentally far away from doing that, I never had the courage, I mean, approaching girls is a struggle for normal people, how can you imagine it was for me?

I felt the energy flowing inside me, the power to change, but am I close to finding myself? I was desperately trying to break the bubble I was in, one scratch at a time, until one day, I had a physiology exam, one of the most detested medical subjects for me, and almost hated by every medical student.

Even though I was well prepared, I worried so much about that exam, but there was that urge in me, an urge telling me not to fail anymore; I can already see myself graduating.

I took the exam in the presence of the head of the department, who was asking me numerous oral questions successfully; I carried on answering all of them. However, I stuttered almost in every answer; it was catastrophic.

Looking at this now, it's obvious for me that I was worried about his opinion and marks rather than concentrating on the questions themselves.

The Clock ticked 15:00.

"You're free to go, Khaled," he told me following my answer to his last question.

"CCCan I know my grade, sir?" I said.

"Khaled, you passed, but I want to tell you something; I suggest you change your major of studies, choose something more manual, using hand skills, where you don't need to talk at all would be better because I am sorry to break it down for you, you're never going be a doctor."

Honestly, I was clueless on how to react to his words; a part of me wanted to tell him it's none of his business, while another part was telling me to hold my respect to him.

I was too young and still too weak; his words hit me like a train, I felt inferior, so inferior.

"Thank you for your advice, sir," I said calmly, but deep inside I was boiling, just like a volcano that is about to erupt.

I left the examination room, and I never saw this professor again.

Why? Why, when I was just starting to break out of those chains, I can already see the cracks on the walls of the bubble surrounding me, but I lost every light hope I once had; I walked my way to my hostel room, drooping in tears and thinking about my future.

"What did you expect? Of course, you're never going to be a doctor with a stutter; have you ever seen a stuttering doctor? You're so absurd," Taurus said.

I was silent all day, listening to him; I was listening and listening and listening even more to every single negative thought that could possibly cross my mind till he had nothing else to say.

He sounded so high yet so shaky; the voice had a resonance of its own, a tone and a pitch just like mine.

He knew perfectly my weaknesses and the exact spot of the chink in my armor; he knew what he was saying; I was so worn out to answer him, I carried my head all the way to my pillow and put my headphones to my ears and went instantly to sleep.

I lost another fight to Taurus.

That day passed.

It was a sad day.

In these hours I've been in bed, I must have woken up six times. Not for that long each time, but enough to break my sleep into un-refreshing chunks. With every disturbance, there is a new nightmare.

Hallucinations, like I've failed my father. My love cheated on me. I never had a real job. The house is burning, and I can't dowse it. I'm running for the bus, but it's pulling away already. My dad's car is sliding on black ice. Then my eyes fell to my feet, the water that pooled was developing ice crystals; my eyes became wider as the crystals spread, merging until it was solid white. Before I could move, my shoes were stuck fast, and from behind came a cold wind. The light began to flicker, then the voice came again, but now right next to my ear.

"Old friend, I've missed you. We're going to have the best time. Why don't you take off your shoes and stand up?" The tips of my cuffs sparked with small flames. A strangled cry rent the air that I only recognized as my own voice when my lungs were empty. I had already stood up and now struggled out of the icy sneakers. Then I turned to face the room. There was no fire, or ashes, or charred logs. The light strobed, and in the dark spells, I caught glimpses of a figure that moved around me, rubbing electric blue hands together.

It felt as if Taurus was sneaking his way into me, manifest all my senses.

Then my bedroom is light, and my mind is moving faster than a three-year-old can speak like it's stuck on fast forward, and the volume is jammed right up. I want to wash my brain in cold water, chill the whole thing right out, but I can't. I want a coffee, but the caffeine will put me over the edge.

I got off the bed and went halfway through the room toward the door as I remember I didn't have breakfast yet;

I look at the time; it was 13:00. I slept for thirteen hours, plus I skipped school. I heard knocks on my door.

As I walked slowly to the door to open it.

"HEY! I am your new roommate."

"Welcome," I said, "make yourself at home."

"There are two other guys I came with I want to introduce you to; they are on the eighth floor," he said.

"Yeah, thank you, not today," I said.

Days passed by, I started to get along with my roommate and the other two guys from the eighth floor; we got really close to each other, we almost spent every day together, we used to fool around constantly, make funny videos, record weird songs, and listen to every new RnB and hip-hop hit on my iPod at that time, our vibes were always positive, at nights we used to gather for a movie in one room, sleepover if needed, every one of us had his own persona, but together we were flawless, we completed one another, this was probably the first time I enjoy having real friends since I left my childhood friends in Abu Dhabi following my father's accident.

By time we formed a crew, more like a brotherhood, we were four, and the devil was our fifth, or perhaps it was in me, I would never know.

We started to rock the city, we went from socializing to partying to recording tracks and throwing concerts, to drug dealing and getting VIP free entries to the city night clubs and to signing autographs by random girls in the streets.

We formed our own fraternity and owned the town; we were called the LPC or, in other words, the lil' pharaohs crew. But before I tell you how we did that, let me tell you how it all started.

At that time, I was starting to discover things about myself I never knew; I was gifted with a good voice and a perfect sense for music; I started getting compliments from close friends and relatives who knew me; singing was one of many getaways from stuttering.

You see, every stutterer can have absolute hundred percent fluency during singing, a miracle, right? I always thought I would make a career out of singing someday.

I used to sing duos with my best friend from my crew, I was the main vocalist singing choruses, and he was just starting his career as a rapper. Currently, he's one of the most known names in the region.

We recorded numerous tracks; we climbed the ladder of fame rapidly, we were getting notable by many in the country, hell, I even sang on stage.

Things started to get really out of hand for me, the world started opening its doors, and the devil took me in his arms; I started to acquire bad habits, I wanted to change, doesn't matter in which direction, I was doing anything to regain my confidence, I changed my outer looks, I was surrounded by bad girls, I let my hair grow for three whole years, I dyed my hair and attended concerts of famous deejays regularly, I looked different and felt different, I didn't realize that I am hiding someone inside of me, I got me some followers who wanted to hang around me, I realized that the worse you become and the faker you get, the more liked by people you turn to be but not the kind of people you want them to stick for long in your life, we used to throw after parties at our house till the morning.

I knew I changed when we used to force newcomers to do filthy deeds just to hang out with us and prove loyalty to our fraternity; I knew I changed when I as soon as I saw someone starting to change for the better, shine in his field, or perhaps become a good student in his class, Taurus would command me to mock him in front of everyone, just to watch him lose his self-confidence one day at a time, stuttering didn't block me from becoming the bully I once hated.

Like a demon enjoying the scene as the trail of blood he made grows thicker, paling the skin of his victims to a translucent white. With each tick of the clock wanting their heart to stop, just stop, to watch their eyes become glassy and vacant. The blood of my last victim had begun to dry, more brownish than scarlet. I was no longer human. Every choice had to lead me here, to the side of the devil.

But in the middle of all of that, a flower bud started appearing in my life when I met this girl who, out of all the girls we knew and hung out with, she was somehow special in her own ways; she saw directly through me, accepted me in all ways, and always saw the good in me. Funny enough to say that apart from all the girls I spoke freely with, she was the one I stuttered with the most.

But falling in love with her was like entering a house and finally realizing I'm home. When she smiled at me, I felt invisible hands wrapping around me, making me feel safe. When her eyes are locked on mine, it's like I can see galaxies instead of just pupils. Having her in my life made me feel like everything's possible in this world like I can conquer anything.

I don't regret meeting her, and I know she might be my first, but what I really wished for is for her to be my last.

Chapter 7
The Loop of Grief

Grasping much reflecting little. Words follow me in tiny crowds, abandon me when needed. The desire to impress her is driving my fingers to type or attempt to type one of these incredibly, or may I say ridiculous sophisticated phrases. Why is it easier here? The flow of words intact, confident yet still in confinement. It's this bittersweet sensation of striving to prove to myself, to her my capabilities, but only to fall victim to my insecurities.

My stutter had created in me a character so insecure; it led me to fall for the first girl that gave me the attention I was looking for; I didn't have much choice. I was hungry for being approved by anyone.

"You should ask her out; you're lucky you got someone who's into you despite your stutter; hold on to her; you never know where you will find someone like this again." Taurus said.

And so, we started dating, I was so young and green, my first relationship and my first love, I lacked a lot of man qualities, the attributes I should've been taught by my father on how to act around women and how to treat them, I was rather a boy, mommy's boy, yet she still wanted to stay with me.

Blind love, lack of character, and stuttering made me quiet not the alpha partner in the relationship; before I even notice she was controlling everything, where we go, where we stay, what we eat, I was nothing but a mere puppet following her.

My first kiss, on a New Year's Eve we spent together with her friends and mine, and before I fly back to my home country for the mid-year school vacation, we gave each other promises that we're going to wait for each other and spend all our life together. Those emotions for this girl, they were new for me; I was hooked, I had so much to tell her, yet my tongue is always turning me down; I was quite sure she got feelings too.

I didn't know why I stuttered awfully with her, it was like every time I wanted to make things better, I just fail to do so and stutter even worse, maybe because I cared so much.

Oceans of emotions, words, and feelings that can't be expressed. Every time we used to go out, I returned home so bitter and mournful, visualizing myself telling her all that I feel, all the words that I am not able to convey.

Her love was making me blind, but after all, I didn't stay blind for long; I had a wake-up call a couple of months following our first date; unfortunately, we don't choose the way we wake up neither do we get warned before, sometimes wake-up calls are rough and heartbreaking.

Eventually, I got cheated on; it was my first heartbreak, a heartbreak that hit me like a train, I heard about betrayals, but I didn't know that the taste of one could be so sour, especially after you give everything you can after you innocently reveal all your cards and show your full true love, I wasn't quite able to interpret where, what and when did I go wrong? What lead to this?

As much as I hated her along with detesting this period of my life and how I did get over this, but I'll always be thankful for this experience; it was a great factor in changing my character since then, while a part of it changed to the better, another part of it forever made me cold-hearted towards women since then.

I remember one day Taurus told me, "Don't ever think a girl will even look at you with your stutter, let alone getting married and having kids."

I recall his words now.

On the other hand, during that episode of my life, Taurus was doing his job perfectly.

"Your expectations were so high."

"You keep forgetting who you are."

"I knew she'd find someone else better than you anyway."

"Look how she's communicating and laughing with your friends. Were you really blind to think she's into you?"

"Forget it, not even worth trying."

It was hard to get over; for several days, these phrases were repeating in my head.

Until one sleepless night at four o'clock in the morning, I went to the bathroom to wash my face, I glanced in the mirror, and gazed at my own reflection.

I saw a miserable human being, a wretched creature, my eyes would roam critically from one feature to another and catalog it in my brain, surprisingly enough, without my own consent I saw myself mumbling his phrases.

That night I saw him. I saw Taurus.

All these years, my own villain was me.

My stutter had led me to create someone in my head that was so dominant to my acts, someone who I thought was always right, someone who knows me better than me, but simultaneously, a worthless creature, a pathetic coward who always desired to be hidden.

By looking in the mirror, I saw Khaled, probably not the Khaled I always dreamed of being, but rather the Khaled I am afraid to be, a nightmare coming true, an animal who's repeatedly trying to eat me alive over and over without losing interest and most importantly a villain who's turning me into a person I refuse to be.

My relationship break-up had caused me huge distress as I always linked it to my stutter; it was a kind of sorrow that touched me somewhere so profound that I never thought I would reach.

After numerous sleepless nights, plenty of attempts from Taurus, who was so persistent in putting me down for a long, long time, I finally answered back.

"You know what, maybe you're right; I'll never really be something in life. I only can dream of being something," I said to him, in a moment of exhaustion and fragility.

I collapsed.

I Surrendered.

It was then and at this exact moment when I stepped foot in the vicious loop of grief.

A loop every stutterer goes through at some point in life, it usually ends with suicidal thoughts if not taken good care of at the right time.

A mental state of speaking with constant fear of stuttering, I spoke, I stuttered, I felt inferior, I got depressed, I spoke again because I have to, I stuttered even worse, I felt more inferior, and I got more depressed, then I speak again and so on.

It's a one-way trip, a loop where there is no way back, only one road out, and it's not a good one.

I reached a place in the loop where I wasn't able to say a word. Just a single word wouldn't come out without massive stuttering and facial seizures.

I ultimately stopped talking, completely stopped.

The world was a dark place for me. I wanted to get out. I didn't know how; I had to live with suicidal tendencies for a while now. I shake my head violently. I pound those roaming thoughts down again and again, but they never seem to dislodge themselves. They will drive me insane. But yet I keep them deep inside, close to my heart they abide. I want to get rid of these terrible thoughts, but I also want to keep them tucked deep inside. They confuse and anger me, and yet they keep on multiplying so fast. They are my worst enemies, yet my closest friends.

I was so deep down there.

No matter what I do, nothing is working out the way I wanted it to be.

I hated my stutter as much as I hated my life.

I started going out on long night walks alone, having this state of mind that I am in an infinite time-lapse, day after day, I wasn't even checking the time, living the day just for the sake of it, all the days seemed the same for me, sometimes I even returned too late to my hostel that they wouldn't open the gates for me thinking I am drunk, maybe I did have the appearances of one, but I was sober. I had to sleep in the cold streets, on the snow, until the next morning.

Suffering alone for days, I made an international call to my mother. I was sure she was the only one who understands me without me saying a word.

"Hello, sweetheart."

"…"

"Darling, are you okay?"

"…"

"It's okay; you can tell me everything."

"I can't talk, Mom…I can't talk."

"I know it's difficult for you, I know life is turning out to be not what you expected, it never was, I've raised you in a way, I was wrong, I was overprotective, I didn't get you exposed to the world while you're with me. Unfortunately, you have to do this with no one around you now; you have to carve your own way, with the tiny little gift God gave you, be in peace with who you are, Khaled, God gave every one of us his full share in life, a hundred percent that is to be divided into various aspects like success, health, love, family, fame, wealth and the list goes on.

God is fair, be sure you'll get your full share and always be grateful for what you have son, remember that I love you more than anyone you met, meet and will meet."

I hung up and burst into tears.

How can I be in peace with a disability?

I was angry at God; why me? Why can't I enjoy talking like all other youth of my age? Why can't I express myself freely? Why me, God? WHY ME?

Chapter 8
The Escape

My jail is just a box for a human, nothing except for the stone-hard bed and the bucket. Those bars are really thick; I know I can't break any of those. Behind me is this foot wide square hole with the same iron bars on it, just like my childhood's bedroom window where it all started, where daylight streams through it. I know that there must be a way; the light from there was like hope. All I had is hope.

What if there was a cure pill? An overnight treatment to end all the suffering? A Dream all stutterers always wish to come true.

Sadly, it's not the way it goes, not for this disability, not for stuttering.

You have to take the tough way, a road full of stones, spikes, and snakes. A path full of sorrow where you must have the competence to lift yourself back up, full of grief where you're forced to get yourself out of it, and full of depressive days which can devour you alive if you let it.

Mother's words were profound.

After calming down, her words were lurking all over my head; I came to realize that I cannot change what and who I am, not in a thousand years; that said, I am still able to change what I want to become.

With Taurus accompanying me, I had two different highways to drive through, either to drown in there and let him take the lead, forever, or shut him down once and for all.

I stepped into the shower, toes flinching as they touched the chilled ceramic floor. My mind was in shreds; I would never get that picture out of my mind when Taurus used to tell me how we'll conquer the world. I turned the dial, old and metallic, releasing thousands of lukewarm drops, darkening my hair, and trickling down my back. My eyes fell closed over and over, each time showing me the scenes I've been through like a movie running on fast forward.

For all the times, I was too afraid to sleep in the dark, staring at my bedroom window since then.

For that life-changing phone call from the hospital and for losing the two human beings I loved the most.

For the time, I innocently tried to introduce myself, panicking and sweating, but all I got is laughs from the people, for the tears that streamed down my face that evening.

For the day I was told I am never going to be a doctor.

For the heartbreak, I got in return for being sincere.

And for all the times I got called "The crippled."

I refused to let go; I held on tight and hanged tough to my timeless dream.

My dream was not to get cured neither to speak fluently.

After being down there, I reached a point that I didn't care anymore about how I talk; the only thing I cared about, is to prove everyone wrong.

I was one inch of giving up when I thought of those who always wanted to see me fail, starting from my own self and my villain, Taurus, to the people who made fun of me, doubted me, and told me I had no future as a doctor, will never attract a girl or even have a family, and the list goes on and on.

My dream was to recover the confidence I once had.

I picked up my sword and chose to fight this battle alone, in a world looking at stutterers with sympathy and categorizing them as the less fortunate in society.

I am worthy of escaping this hurricane of thoughts, the positive and the negative analysis of the actions and words of others. I am worthy of love and a better life. I am.

And so I make my escape plan through the paths of musical lyrics and stories of adventure, through the green leaves and under open skies. Looking at Taurus in the eye, Stuttering wasn't my center of attention anymore, and that's exactly when my life started to change.

Chapter 9
Rebirth

"Khaled, we're going for a shawarma, come with me."

"But you're not here, Dad."

"I am right behind you, son, right behind you."

I looked behind me, seeing a very bright light shining from my window.

Waking up can be really harsh, especially if your dreams are better than reality. The saddest part of it is that eventually, even the memory of your dream will fade. If you are even lucky enough to remember it, that is. Then you're left with this lonely feeling of detachment, left to explore in the empty void of emotions, the only proof that you ever had the dream, to begin with.

I wake the way kings wake, just the same. We are all blessed with the same time, the same experience of consciousness. My eyes greet the day shine, my heart and lungs expand. There are times that I feel that I must have been so blessed to live the same day over and over, even though I age, for those first few moments are so identical. At first, there are the dreams, then the sense of welcoming a new day, the anticipation of whatever comes.

And so, I started to open my eyes to the blessings I have, the things I once took for granted. Things that people would die to have, I started to look at the half-full cup.

I took my shirt off and looked at my own reflection in the mirror. I was overweight at the time; my hours and hours of gaming, eating fast food, having sleeping disorders, and not following a proper diet had lead me to gain a lot of weight after being the athlete kid I used to be back in the days.

I realized that I need to put myself back on track and get my body back in shape. I began to treat my body right; I educated myself, read books, watched videos, and learned from trainers and nutritionists, started all the way from the bottom, from making a gym training program to myself, a diet plan, and a lifestyle I was abiding by.

On one beautiful day, I read about a marathon of twelve kilometers that was going to be held in two months. I got myself a new running shoes and started preparing for it as I should, some days I was motivated, some days I wasn't, but I was improving each and every day, doing my daily runs even in heavy rains and cold snows, I can still feel those snowflakes hovering around me and enter through my nostrils as I raise the pace of my speed and progressing day after day.

Witnessing my weight falling and my body composition change dramatically, the marathon day arrived, I managed to nail a twelve kilometres with a record of 52 minutes 17 seconds, by time, I had carved the body of my dreams and made a major body transformation at the age of twenty-four.

Being overjoyed with my first accomplishment, I was starting to get requests to coach, write diet plans, and help people get the body they dream of.

I had to coach people of different ages and genders; they trusted me with their money, time, and most importantly their bodies. I had a good confidence boost. A fuel that pushed me further to different success paths I was curious to discover.

This little jump start was a path set to start taking other aspects of my life more seriously.

Women, at a point in my life were a red zone, a zone I was always afraid to get close to; simply the fact of approaching a woman and start a conversation would make me shake like a leaf and would make my anxiety levels hit the roof.

I was in constant exploration for new quests; one of my main challenges at the time was how to simply attract women, how to approach them, what to say, and how to say it; the stutter always multiplied the difficulty of what I wanted to achieve, but I always had the mindset of "the more it's difficult the more I want to do it". Then another goal was set.

I started reading various self-help books, books about dating and approaching women, hearing multiple audiobooks until I came across an ultimate mentor who taught me a lot during my voyage with women, his teachings were unique, and it fitted me on a personal level as a stutterer far beyond only success with women. While all other gurus in the dating field were talking about pickup lines and how to get a girls number, this guy was building his focus on how to improve one's inner game before his outer game, how to transform from a boy to a man, and above all the ability to detach and keep oneself together regardless of what's happening in his life.

As much as he was very successful, I always felt he was talking to me, as his seminars were so profound regarding confidence. He affirmed that women would naturally feel attracted without even you noticing if you practiced what he preaches. Because at the end of the day, as he always said, "Attraction is not a choice."

After applying his perspective on my life and my previous failed relationship, I started relating to what he said, I started changing, or in other words, I was feeling that stage of evolution from a small little mommy's nice boy and how that's always been a major turn off for every woman I encountered, to a man, a man fully responsible of his actions and never throwing blame on people and circumstances, more importantly, never throwing blame on a stutter. I started to accept everything.

I was in a life-changing phase of my character, my confidence was indeed higher, and my charisma had an aura of its own in any place I would go.

My dating mentors were right; women's attention was automatically drawn towards me without even me approaching them; they didn't even know I stutter until I actually do approach them.

My approaches were different; I learned to be counter-intuitive and witnessed how women adore that. I also learned that it is absolutely okay to get rejected by some women, and that has absolutely nothing to do with me or with my stutter; even the best-looking men get rejected. I stopped allowing that to reflect on my inner self-esteem like before; for me, it was either their win or their loss after all.

The dating field always had that question, "what do women really want?" I cannot say I got the answer for that, but I got a tailored answer just for me, an answer that perfectly fitted how I see and interact with them.

After seeing my growth reflect proportionally on my confidence, I realized that the more I try to hide my stutter, the more I actually do stutter, so I started to use it for my own good.

"Hey, I know you're into me."

"Oh really, how?"

"That look you just gave me."

"What look?"

"The look you gave me when I just stuttered! Stop playing with your hair."

And they just burst into laughter.

A fragment of how I embraced my stutter that women actually were convinced it's sexy.

I have made many approaches and pickups by then, including a very famous female deejay I met in one party I was at; she was the glamorous type; she knew that she got it all and was perfectly aware of that, playing music for hundreds at the time, probably thousands now, just when every other man in the club viewed her as the prohibited fruit and automatically pictured her as a higher status than their selves, placing her on a high pedestal and making her unattainable, me, on the other hand, I viewed her as a normal girl who's just doing her job. I approached her right after she finished playing, between the eyes of all the lurking men there, and since then, we became very close friends.

The trust I got from mastering communication skills with the other sex had pushed me to further borders, and with every accomplishment, there was a further boost in my self-recognition. It naturally raised the platform of my confidence and lowered the platform of my stutter just like an old weighing scale.

As I saw my life slowly and steadily pacing on the right track, I still had that evil side of me coming every once in a while. Taurus didn't like it. That trust I am giving to myself again, that confidence.

I've been insisting on ignoring him, mute myself when his whispering comes, but the voices came again that day while am sitting alone enjoying my cup of tea and reading my anatomy atlas.

"I'm still here."

"No you're not. You're gone, you're not even real Taurus"

"I'm not entirely sure what I am. I can sense, but not in the way I once did. I see but not like before. You think your success attracts me? You're wrong, such things repulse me. You know I can help you. I can take all that stuff away so that you can be like me. When you join me, we'll return together like before, though really, I haven't found an end to it yet. Should we lose each other, the isolation begins again, and I must liberate you one more time. Step away from the ugly form you are becoming. Come to me, my old friend."

His intonation seemed weak. I could sense his vulnerability. He wasn't able to comprehend the abrupt motive that boosted me to transform for the better. I didn't let myself fall to his words. Neither was I that strong as I seemed. I still returned to him in the days where my stutter failed me. Just as a boy runs to his dad, I still was dependent on his power, and from time to time, I still had remnants of evil shattered inside of me, I still enjoyed watching successful people sink in despair and lose their faith in their selves.

It wasn't long until I met my true love.

By April that year, I would have completed quite enough time to know a girl, a girl that was very close to my heart.

It's funny how a girl thinks it's a relationship after three dates but a guy thinks it's a relationship after several months. They just go with the flow, let each day build a picture until they feel certain that when they are with you, they are a better and happier version of themselves. And that's smart if you think about it. You can only ever get to know a person over time. It's when you are comfortable together and real, when you talk in a way best friends do, only then, you know that things are right.

She was the kind of girl that women loved to hate. She was an adult, I suppose, but so young that she still had the exuberance of youth. She had that movie star look, not overly tall and willowy, but more like an action star. Her muscle definition was perfect, and she walked with the confidence of someone a decade older. She wasn't just flawless in her bone structure, her skin was like silk over glass, and she radiated an intelligent beauty.

We were young and crazy, we used to go to the moon to have fun, only to realize that the moon was not as fun as we were.

Judging my life at that time, I decided to be a man and put a ring on the girl that was always there for me.

I proposed to the love of my life, in an unforgettable moment of joy and happiness that will forever be carved in my heart; I got married in June later on that year then continued the rest of my life as a young husband with my lifetime partner, Marina.

Although I have always been indecisive about having kids, the idea of creating a big family was the first thing in my mind after marriage, to be responsible for someone and to pass on what I've learned and what is yet to learn to other generations, however, just like every step you take as an adult you need to be financially ready for it. And while I am on a trial to survive financially, I decided to try my luck in the industry.

I dug deep in my dreams and came up with that one business idea, that one thing that always linked me with my father, the things we both loved to eat.

I chose to partner with a friend to open up a small shawarma spot right next to my university which started off pretty well. I used to have all the students eating at my spot daily, I started from scratch, waking up at five o'clock in the morning every day to get the food cooked and ready to be served at nine sharp, I stood by myself serving people of different ages and nationalities. I managed my time between school and my food store without skipping classes, my partner and I made a schedule that suited both of us.

As soon as we started growing, became stable enough for the place to stand on its feet, I hired employees to run it for me, a professional cook, and two waitresses, a staff whom I learned a lot from, by having employees under my command, my first experience not only as a boss who points out at things and yells all the time, which I normally did from time to time, but as a ship captain commanding the hull, who understood quite well that my employees and I are in the same boat, and if someone fell, evidently all of us will.

People adored the spot; while having four more competitors in the region, I had to always outwork others, be creative about the taste and the cost. I've put myself in an industry where the level of competition is relatively high; I reached my break-even point by the third month, which was the fastest-growing shawarma store in town.

My stutter was always there, some days I didn't feel it, some days I did, my phone was always ringing with calls, I was speaking all the time, ordering stocks and beverages from the suppliers to keep my store running.

Until one day, the town hall decided to close all the food spots in the area for some reason, it was a sad day, my partner and I tried negotiating with the government hoping to keep our place alive, but we failed, we had to make a fast decision, either we close for good and sell our equipment or invest in another place.

Refusing to back down, our next plan was to upgrade from a small kiosk to a restaurant; we found a place not that far from our first spot. I invested all of my previous saved revenues in the new restaurant, decorations, interior designs, and expensive cooks. The business ran perfectly the first couple of months, but it was never as successful as the old store.

Unfortunately, it wasn't long till the business took the downslide and started running on negative costs. Lack of business background and social experiences was vital for such a big step, I used to add up from my own pocket money on trying to resuscitate it, but it never came back to life again.

Days, weeks, and months of sleepless nights, the effort put, debts rising in hope for it to revive, but it didn't, it was dead, until one day I walked into the restaurant, I gazed at the place that was once crowded with students, today it was like an abandoned desert. It wasn't long till I decided to call it off.

My decision to stop was typically in the perfect time. A couple more weeks my debts would've been doubled. I put up my restaurant for sale, I got myself a buyer a couple of days later on, he seemed elegant and gentle, and most of all he looked rich and had big plans for the place, it's a pity, I got deceived, and all of that turned out to be a shabby mask which fell off right after we signed the contract.

I was so naive back in the days, thinking all the people are good, I trusted everyone just by their looks. I lacked so much social intelligence as my stutter led to a shortfall in communication with a lot of people throughout the years.

And so, I got scammed for a serious amount of money, and I never saw the elegant and gentleman again.

It surely was an amazing ride. The life lessons I learned were priceless, my character evolved to become more balanced and reliable, and my business background dredged.

On the other hand, I felt that life gave me a hard slap to the face and revealed its true side. It was proving to me that it's not always rainbows and butterflies. Not all people are as good as I thought, as good as my mother raised me.

No question, I fell into a small period of depression following that important amount of money loss; I lingered in my room for a couple of days, refused to talk to anyone, but could it really be that bad? Haven't I already been to the baseline of depression? I've probably seen it all, and I know what's down there. As much as this incident severed me, deep inside, I knew I am just getting started.

I came home that night, and my wife was sitting on the couch with tears on her face. She looked at me as soon as I stepped home. I can see she's hiding something behind her back. I approached her gently and hugged her, asked her what's wrong; she was hiding that urine pregnancy test in her right hand, showing two red sticks.

"I'm pregnant," she said with her eyes full of tears.

I looked at her, laughed, and hugged her. At that moment, my arms squeezed a fraction tighter, and she breathed more slowly. I felt her body melting into mine as every muscle lost its tension to the spring air.

"Stupid, what are you laughing at," she told me while hitting me with her weak cute hands on my chest.

"We're ready for this," I told her and kissed her.

It's like she was waiting for these words. She calmed down and hugged me so tight, and then she slept like a baby that night.

But I didn't; I was sleepless.

I remembered that I read some articles about stuttering being inherited, that there are studies and worldwide statistics proving it. My only worry was for my child to grow up with a stutter, for him to experience what I suffered, what am I enduring, and will yet to go through.

"Too early to be thinking about that, Khaled," I whispered to myself.

I chose not to worry about that for now and decided to focus on the more important things in my life at that period. I took a vow not to think about it.

And so, when my thoughts became nonsense, and all the more interesting for it, I knew I was falling asleep.

Now all I had to do was let go.

I hugged my wife and closed my eyes; as my consciousness ebbed, my mind went into free fall, swirling with the beautiful chaos of a new dream.

Chapter 10
My Soul Doesn't Stutter

Rediscovering self has always been one of my favorite endeavors, and well, you might question as to how can it be so, for rediscovery for normal people is mostly a once or, if they really need it, a twice in a lifetime thing. Yet to me, it is something I tend to strive for every now and then, something I do for the sake of the journey. For me, the process is like an unknown path each time I travel down upon it. Yes, the fellow travelers I bump into along the way are mostly the same each time, but that track differs in each such attempt. Once, it even seemed to me like being in a sort of trance and living for a while all in memoriam whilst examining various pearls from that wonderful casket. It is true exhilaration.

I am now bouncing back, looking for another adventure, another challenge to prove to myself that stuttering is actually not a thing, a never-ending battle between Taurus and me about who's going to take the lead of my life.

As if learning a new language, mastering it like native speakers, and speaking it almost like my mother tongue wasn't a challenge enough for someone who's stuttering in his own native voice.

Or perhaps having a wife and a son at a young age, taking full responsibility wasn't a challenge enough.

I wasn't satisfied. I was in total acceptance of every dare that's coming my way.

And so, six years of medical school were coming to an end. It was the time to take my final exam for all the subjects I studied for six years, an exam determining my future title, meaning so much to me, setting the note for my future strides, and proving some people wrong.

Preparing for the exam had me stressed out for a few weeks, which relatively led my stutter to increase. However, three weeks later, I was standing right there, looking just as I imagined I would look like at my graduation ceremony.

It was finally here. The moment of truth, the stepping stone to the real world. This was what they've been preparing us for. After six memorable years. Through the good, bad, idiotic, fun, and change. It was finally time, time to step out into that bright light, shake the hand of an administrator, and grab the ticket to freedom. The piece of paper that would remind me forever that I've accomplished something, all I had to do was sit in this uncomfortable robe and wait for my name to be called.

Breathing out my last words as a student and abiding by the oath of Hippocrates.

"I swear to fulfill, to the best of my ability and judgment, this covenant:

"I will respect the hard-won scientific gains of those physicians in whose steps I walk and gladly share such knowledge as is mine with those who are to follow.

"I will apply, for the benefit of the sick, all measures that are required, avoiding those twin traps of overtreatment and therapeutic nihilism.

"I will remember that there is an art to medicine as well as science and that warmth, sympathy, and understanding may outweigh the surgeon's knife or the chemist's drug.

"I will not be ashamed to say "I know not," nor will I fail to call in my colleagues when the skills of another are needed for a patient's recovery.

"I will respect the privacy of my patients, for their problems are not disclosed to me that the world may know. Most especially must I tread with care in matters of life and death. If it is given to me to save a life, all thanks. But it may also be within my power to take a life; this awesome responsibility must be faced with great humbleness and awareness of my own frailty. Above all, I must not play at God.

"I will remember that I do not treat a fever chart, a cancerous growth, but a sick human being, whose illness may affect the person's family and economic stability. My responsibility includes these related problems if I am to care adequately for the sick.

"I will prevent disease whenever I can, for prevention is preferable to cure.

"I will protect the environment which sustains us, in the knowledge that the continuing health of ourselves and our societies is dependent on a healthy planet.

"I will remember that I remain a member of society, with special obligations to all my fellow human beings, those sound of mind and body as well as the infirm.

"If I do not violate this oath, may I enjoy life and art, respected while I live and remember with affection thereafter. May I always act so as to preserve the finest traditions of my calling, and may I long experience the joy of healing those who seek my help."

I can proudly say, I am now a doctor.

"Hello, mom, just wanted to tell you that I love you, you always had my back, and today I am a doctor because of you."

It was the first phone call I made with my gown on.

I dashed to the office of my physiology professor to show him my diploma, the man who with certainty once declared to me that I would never be a doctor. Unluckily, he wasn't there.

My lovely wife was already in her third trimester at the time; she was there witnessing my graduation. It was a moment of pride, honor, and grace to those who believed and saw through me. I thought that was everything to achieve though it was only the kick-off to my career.

With the accouchement knocking doors, there was always a mysterious link between me and my boy since he was in his mother's womb, makes me remember every time when I had a fight with Marina, resulting in some cruel words coming from her side in moments of anger, where I just have to end the conversation, I go spend some time with myself, sit alone, angry, sad, every once in a while shedding a few tears, I usually get calls from her five minutes later, howling; he's moving and kicking potently inside there, while I come to soothe her big belly, I start to calm down, so does he and the pain just fade away.

Two months later, the moment finally came, those tiny fingers curled around my pinky. I watched him peer through brand new eyes at what must be such a strange world after life in the womb. His legs kick in a tiny jagged motion, looking for that resistance they are used to I guess, but finding nothing but air. I wonder if that's unsettling or a relief, it must have been pretty cramped in there. When he stretches, his hands barely rise above his head, and I think of how strange we'd all look if we kept those body proportions as we grew. He begins to fret and cry, everyone tells me how annoying that's going to be, but it's so adorable I almost cry.

Adam was born, I was there, right next to my wife during labor, holding her hands in every breath and crying just as much as her when I first saw him, since then and until now, Adam's feelings were always profound, he's humble, and his love is so innocent.

I became a young father at the age of twenty-four, I had mixed feelings, delight mixed with worry, that burden, how am I supposed to raise a child while I myself am still a student in this big world, will I be able to give him advice, how will he look at my stuttering, what will I tell him? I wanted him to be perfect, just like every father wants his son to be.

Following through the annual ritual, visiting my mother back in Egypt every year, they were overjoyed with my first son, Karim, my elder brother was treating him like his, and Adam by time was learning a lot from him, they developed a boy-uncle link I couldn't intervene between, but I was contented.

However, this year, Egypt was different, my home country was going through a huge revolution against their dictator at that time, the Egyptians have had enough, and the whole world was talking about us, while the media doesn't show the full side of the story, I came back that year and laid eyes on my beautiful city, I saw wrecked streets, families losing their youth, fathers being arrested and put in jails, the typical price that had to be paid for confronting a dictator.

Although I was always detached from the dirty games of politics but seeing young people from my own race in the daily news losing their lives was killing me.

I prepared a small medical kit and used to go to the main square of our protests to volunteer as a field doctor; even with my not-so-big experience yet at the time, I was glad I was a reason to save some lives.

It was the first time I experience life-death situations right in front of my eyes, I hated politics since then, and I hated the devils wearing the faces of humans who were a reason for all of that.

Flying back to Ukraine to move on with my life, the search for a new challenge was still running in my blood. I was thirsty for being better, getting richer mentally, and subsequently getting more and more confident. By that time, I was starting to realize that my stuttering is diminishing. I even met people I know who inquired about it.

"Hey Khaled, when did you get treated?"

"How and what did you do?"

Actually, I did nothing.

I have learned one fact by now, that one of the keys to reducing stuttering is being in total ignorance to the fact that it's here in the first place and rather focusing on self-improvement, forever and always.

By that time, I felt I was missing something, a sport that would improve me as a whole, accentuate my qualities and make me a part of a team.

Until this cold November day arrived, while doing my routinely workout in the gym and just after am done with bench pressing, I was approached by a super muscular and fit guy of my age.

"I have been witnessing your body transformation and weight improvement for a very long time. You're doing a great job" he said.

"Thhhanks, I aaappreciate that."

"Here is my card; our practice is next Tuesday, at the stadium, I would like to see you there."

"What sport iiis that?" I asked.

"American football."

I went back home, thinking about the offer, and spoke with my wife about it, telling her how this is going to touch my stutter positively.

Before I make up my mind to go, I decided to attend a live game on a Saturday night.

As soon as I entered the stadium, you could feel the adrenaline from the pitch to the stands and flowing right around the stadium. It was the sort of tension people crave because it comes right before the elation. Maybe there is something about that, the possibility of joy rather than the certainty that makes it all so much fun. I wonder if it comes from the days of humans hunting that when they caught their prey, the joy came as an ecstasy. And here we are, these teams giving us the chance to feel tribal, to feel the ancient part of us emerge and dance.

And so, I went to the first practice, since then, I was captured in the scent of it, and I didn't leave, I fell in an everlasting love with the game.

While stuttering, trying to prove myself in a team full of Russians and Ukrainians wasn't a piece of cake and while I am the only foreigner in the history of the team, proving myself to the coaches wasn't an easy job either, as football is all about how you interact with your team and read each other.

Just like every other sport I played since childhood, I shined right away. I became the starting linebacker for three consecutive years. I managed to win and get nominated for various trophies annually, in conjunction with Rookie of the year, most improved player, and most valuable player, to say the least.

I identified my own self in every aspect of the game, in every quality football adds to your character, perseverance, goal-setting, handling failure as well as success, it enlightened me to work hard but always play smart, physical and mental strength was the key to a lot of things, patience too, respect to your mentors, to play through pain and never ever to give up, it taught me time management particularly that I was trying to always balance between work, home, and practices, last but not least I learned that I couldn't win all the time, no one does, ever.

But above all of that and as time went by, I gained a great life asset from football, its leadership.

That ought to be a billion-dollar industry. Managers all over the world pay for leadership training, and they pay to learn how to lead themselves. Coaches lead teams, but only to a certain extent. Me, I started as a small leader who encourages his teammates when the score isn't in their favor.

Leadership is learned in many ways, and in football, it's learned early. I learned to lead and motivate others by example, an asset, I didn't know that it would come in hand later on in my life and that I'll forever be grateful for football as a reason.

The fuel to my stuttering was greatly boosted. The confidence and self-esteem were at their peak. Football was and will always remain one of the main factors of self-confidence, which keeps me running until now.

Days, months, and years passed, and although I never reached the point of full recovery, stuttering was not an issue for me. Yes, I stuttered from time to time. Taurus was in constant trials of putting me down, doing his thing.

And so, following my graduation, I carried on with my studies to open more horizons. I chose to do my master's degree in a specialty I always dreamed of, but before I tell you which field was it and how did it go, let me tell you how I met a brother and how I will never forget that day; the day when I was walking in the university campus, and a young man approached me, possibly a freshman.

"Hello!"

"HHHHey, can I help you?" I answered.

"C-C-Can you please t-t-tell me where is the pharmacy c-c-campus."

I was silenced for a couple of seconds, waiting for him to repeat what he said so I could make sure that he's really one of them, one of us.

"I am a-a-asking if you know w-w-w-where the ph-pharmacy campus is."

"Yes, it's rrrright through the gggates on your llllleft hand."

We smiled at each other; he thanked me and left.

It was the first time in my life to meet a stutterer, there was a day where I thought I would never meet someone like me. I believe fate brought us together in the same place at the same time.

Since then, we became friends, periodically seeing one another in the university campus and grab a drink together. We had a lot of gossips, shared life situations, the occurrences we've been through, and the first disappointing reactions from the people. Our adventures were almost identical. I felt I was speaking with my own self; we understood each other like no other. I felt home.

Some days I think, meeting someone new is a divine pleasure. Regardless of how things turn out, I love the dance that begins. The most important idea is to be able to get a true feeling for who they are over a few weeks and months without ever forming an opinion of them. You let them develop as an old polaroid photograph, nice and slow. Perhaps they are a lifelong friend, a lovable rogue, or a person too damaged to give in an emotionally warm and nurturing way.

I remember there was a time I spent a lot of hours reading about different types of stutterers, the repetitive, the prolongation, and the blocks type. I knew for myself that I fall under that prolongation type of stutterers. As much as I hated it, especially when I used to say my name introducing myself and I happen to stutter in it, a prolongation of "Kh" would almost seem like I am about to spit, funny isn't it. Obviously, he was the repetitive type. Meeting a different stutter pattern was very interesting for me to see.

Although life threw us to different places now, it has always been a pleasure to have a drink with him every now and then; meeting him was a reminder that I am not alone.

So, my new friend, all I can say is I am glad we met.

By this time, I seemed so strong from the outside, but I was always in constant struggle with Taurus from the inside, a side no one ever knew, even the closest ones.

Having been studying for my masters always got me stressed back then. It was draining a lot of energy, time, and even money.

Career-wise, it was about time I do my first ever summary presentation on the subject theme of my master's project I've been working on in order to get accepted to proceed.

As usual, I have done a lot of preparations, numerous rehearsals; I was full of myself knowledge-wise; however, my confidence was a little shaky, I doubted my tongue, I sensed it was going to betray me, I was skeptical.

After enough reciting and repeating the same speech over and over again in front of the mirror with absolute no stutter, the day of my presentation had finally come.

The Hall was massive. It was almost half full of professors and heads of various medical departments, old and young doctors, men and women of different ages and from different hospitals, all of them came today, they were eager to listen to me, and to a couple more young doctors who also had to present their studies.

And like the good old days, the game of turns commenced. If it was me to choose, I would've chosen to be the first; unluckily, the choice was not mine. I kind of knew and was quite sure what waiting for my turn will do to me and how sorely it will affect me.

Yes, I was chosen to be the last.

Waiting for a moment to come to just speak and give an impression were always a pain I didn't want to go through; it always provoked Taurus to come out and pull me down to his abyss, it lingers my brains to stray imagining all these terrible scenarios that might and would happen as soon as I begin spelling a few words.

With a mumbling voice in my head telling me that I am going to mess things up, Taurus voice was getting higher and louder every time my turn gets closer; in a couple of minutes, I found myself sweating, having a fast and bizarre breathing pattern, and for the first time I was encountering true chest pain.

It's the panic attack I almost forgot about. I almost forgot how does that feel.

Sadly, I allowed fear and doubt to enter me once again, and no matter what I did at that moment, panic never left me; following that, a frenzy was activated, and Taurus was uncontrollable. I wanted to leave, but it was late, too late.

All at once, I felt that all that I built in the previous five years has turned to ashes. In a blink of an eye, my confidence levels got nullified de novo, and Taurus overtook me once again, and although I discerned before I rise on that stage that it's going to end badly, I still didn't turn back; deep down, I didn't want to give in to Taurus.

But he won regardless.

The hall turned blurry when I was up there. I didn't see the fifty-plus doctors and professors at that time, neither did I saw all the preparing and rehearsing I did for weeks; the view from the stage was black, there was no one to cheer for me in the seats, I only saw my stuttering self, I saw Taurus in the back seat looking at me while I was on stage.

Just like ants run to hide back in their cave when they sense danger, in mere seconds, I returned to the bubble where I once belonged.

My stutter went wild. Words were insanely hard to come out, convoyed with body jerks and face twitches, talking about the full stutter package here, classic.

As much as I was determined to go up there and talk, I got bruised in the end. It was crazy, just like hitting your head to a concrete wall expecting not to bleed. I was up there for forty minutes when I should've been taking a ten to fifteen minutes project presentation, reminiscing the memories of my first day of school. It was just a typical situation as the one I had back then, however, this time as a grown-up rather than a twelve-year-old kid.

"Let's call it off. I agree with his master's theme. Let's vote for approval," said the head of the professors as he chimed in my presentation.

The majority voted yes, and I got approved to start my master's project.

I descended from the stage, and the presentation was over. Forty minutes of hell which seemed to pass more like four hours. Everyone left, but I stayed in the hall room for some time. I was alone, not knowing, what's happening, what just happened, and what's going to happen in the future. How did I get so down again? What made him get through me? How was I not able to control it as I did before?

Too many questions lurking in my head, fear of the future was always there no matter how strong I felt. There is something about public speaking that always got me on my knees, something that makes me so vulnerable.

My morals definitely weren't at their peak at that time. I felt so down, I did cry, but I promised myself I would get up. It's okay to cry, and it's okay to feel that sorrow. What is not okay is to let it go through you. The choice was mine.

But I have already learned this lesson, I learned to shed some tears, get sad for some time and get back up again, it's like I am taking a break, or perhaps a breath, a moment of weakness, before returning to my full power, I knew deep inside that I lost a battle, but I didn't lose the war.

After hovering in my concavity for a couple of days and after calming down and recollecting my feelings, I started to see all of this with a clear state of my mind and from a different perspective, if it's one lesson I learned it's that *the fear of stuttering can easily become worse than stuttering itself.*

I finally admitted to myself that I had a problem with public speaking; a goal was then set to overcome this, with whatever it takes from mental and psychological strength.

I've always thought that setting goals well comes from a soulful meditation, a profound sense of why I am alive and what I wish to give. Added to that, I found the obstacle to my own success when I realized it was something I was either doing or not doing, that I had the power to make changes that were positive. Just like a great athlete who gets there by choosing to train every day because they listened to their inner passion, and this was the whispering of their soul. A great writer who writes every day because at the deepest level of who they are, there is a flourishing of words that need to be born into the world and live in the hearts of others to bring health and joy. A builder or engineer who lives to solve puzzles in three-dimensional space, to provide shelter, a place to call home. A mathematician who lives to solve theorems gives answers that fuel technological innovations.

And so the way forward is to find this inner wish, this innate desire, and passion, and then see how to scale or walk around your obstacle, to dance that exact path you feel compelled to dance. Then every day, you take steps toward conquering it, for, over time, those steps take you to your goal and even beyond it to new horizons. This is growth, and the focus you need comes easily when it is born of your loving curiosity, a sense that if you achieve, you benefit everyone else, that you will have a beautiful gift to give others. Your wish, your love, your curiosity, your desire to help others, your need to be your true self.

That was my "why?"

I took an oath "one day, you Khaled, will make a speech where you will listen to the applaudisments of the audience ringing in your ears like a melody, everyone in the crowd will clap for you and respect you the way you deserve to be respected."

The egg yolk sun poured through the cracks in the blind and awaited entrance into my eyes. Sight still in the clutches of the night's glue, I hesitantly rubbed the dreams away.

Thoughts of the visions in sleep come and go in waves, clinging on to the very last memory of the night, but with little success, I woke up this morning with the overwhelming news of my wife's pregnancy with my second baby. This time it's a girl. I knew her name before I even think about it.

Chapter 11
Nour

Newborn cries fill the room, and I burst into tears of relief and joy. I turn my glossy eyes to my wife, and in a voice that's almost broken, I tell her we have a beautiful daughter. Through her exhaustion, she smiles, and she lets her eyes leave my face to take in the baby that is being brought to lay on her bare skin. At that moment, she begins to cry the sweetest tears she's ever known, all the pain of moments before melting away. She's only minutes old, and her tiny girl begins to root, mouth wide, her instincts strong.

A Light was re-shed on me once again. Nour was born five months later.

She was the joy of my life, a light that was cast off in a time of gloom, hence her name. I saw my sister in her eyes, her every movement, every look, and every touch when she held my finger with her cute little hands. I was blessed once again.

Months passed by, and I got myself back on track again, doing my thing in football, personal coaching in the gym, and working on my master's graduation project. I never stopped educating myself and gaining knowledge in every life aspect. I was regularly reading self-help books about leadership and confidence. I was always listening to audiobooks on my iPod, in my car, or even at home. I got myself new life coaches and great mentors. I was always guided, never lost sight of my goal.

Just like every couple, problems started to arise between my wife and me. After all, a young couple with two kids did not seem to be an easy job; we were fussing and fighting over the tiniest things possible. Stuttering was getting harsh when I used to get nervous, raise my voice, or try to prove a point in a heated conversation; sometimes it was so bad that I just quit trying to prove my point, saving myself time and energy, which was never a good thing to do as a stutterer, it always backfired a couple of days after, leaving me in an even worse inner mood as I surrender to not expressing myself, my feelings and my anger.

Three years through my master's program, the day of my final presentation was getting closer and closer. With all that I have in mind is how I embarrassed myself in the last presentation, what will I do this time?

I was still not ready to go up there; something mysterious was still missing, something that will allow me to communicate, carefree, something I will get introduced to one day, but not now.

I came up with a temporary plan for my show. I hired a colleague who would stand with me on stage doing the reading part, while I, on the other hand, will be ready to answer any questions that arise during and following the presentation.

I thought I shouldn't keep bumping my head to the wall. After all, maybe there can be a way around it to reach the same destination. A temporary solution, at least for now.

The final presentation day had arrived, surprisingly, in the same hall as the last one; however, not the same attendees, they were even more, much more.

And then another game of turns bowled, doing my best to totally disengage myself mentally from the hall and the audience while waiting for my turn.

All of the noise disappeared in an instant. It was like being stuck between two realities, one that was imperfect but doable. The other the vision where I pictured myself, the one I longed myself to be a part of. Was it a possibility to make that world into reality? The only thing that separated me from achieving the dream was myself; and so, I've managed to put Taurus on mute.

Thinking about how fast I want to come back home to play with Nour as soon as possible and as much as I hated waiting, this time I didn't feel the minutes, the clock ran fast and my turn came faster, I was glad.

And here I am on stage, "Ladies and gentlemen, I am Dr. Khkhkhaled Bassyouny, because of my stutter and as I rrrrespect your precious time, mmmmy colleague here is going to ppppresent the ssstudies. Hhhhowever I'll be glad to answer any of yyyyour questions dddduring or after the ppppresentation."

I can't recall that I stuttered much at that time.

The idea was well accepted by the audience, and many questions were raised following the presentation, which I answered flawlessly.

Most people think of a stammer as one where the first letter of a word gets repeated before the word is finally spit out. Some think a stammer is a sign of nerves. Others think it's because you don't know what you want to say. But for me, none of those things are true. I know what I want to say. And after some years I think I know how to say it, and instead of repeating the first consonant, I tend to have a long, drawn-out silence before I say anything at all.

It was probably the first time I acknowledge my stutter in front of a group of people. I usually always try to camouflage it; however, since then, this was a key to many approaches in my speeches in the future, it decreased my anxiety and constant fear that people would find out about my stutter, it kind of put me in control of the situation.

After answering the questions thrown at me every now and then, the presentation was over.

A half victory, or so I would call it, a tricky one maybe, I was tackling the goal, not the main problem, but sometimes we need to look for different ways to reach the destination we want to, and maybe postpone fixing the same path we take for the time when we know how and what to do exactly to fix it, when we know we're ready.

Two weeks later, I became a specialist in my field. I was a Surgeon.

Thinking about that now, every success I achieved had cost me a lot, a lot of stuttering, blocks, doubts, tears, and life lessons all the way. Despite all the odds, so far, I've cut a long way with stuttering, I've seen things I've never expected to see, and I've achieved the things I put my head to. I was so proud of myself, my close ones were proud of me, and most importantly, my mother was over the sky.

Stuttering was and will always be my best friend and my worst enemy, the motive that keeps that flame burning inside of me to prove to myself in this big world that I am not different than any other, and also the enemy that stops me whenever it is more powerful. An amazing love-hate ratio to be noted.

After finishing almost ten years of medical studies, with all of their good and bad moments, it was time to look for a real job, time to earn some money and raise the living of my family, but not here, after I finished my masters, me and my wife had a long conversation and decided to move back to Egypt, and continue our life there.

And so by the end of July that year, we started packing slowly and steadily until the travel day came.

It was two o'clock in the morning when I was packing my final accessories in my backpack.

In this backpack was my world, my everything, all heaved onto shoulders that look too frail to bear it. It has seen better days, frayed around the piping. My wife always says I should get another, but I love this one too much. We've been on so many adventures together this fabric and I, my worldly goods of all my previous journeys are safe inside. So if it breaks a little, I'll simply sew it up, reinforce the weaknesses and keep on moving. By the end, it will be more technicolor than any dream-coat and mean as much to me as anything ever could.

Our plane was scheduled at six, and my wife and kids decided to take a nap before I wake them up for a long journey when Taurus showed up as I seal my backpack.

"You won't find a job. Who would want a stutterer to work for him anyway? Can you even imagine yourself in an interview?" he said.

"Yes, I do, strong and confident," I answered.

"You've changed," Taurus replied.

"I don't know, but it's time to move on. I am still afraid, I've been fighting on my own for too long, and you don't seem like you're coming back," I whispered as I got up and perched my backpack to my back like a little koala to its mother.

Taurus came as an ambassador for my own self. He came to speak of the pain he could not articulate, to break him out of his coma. For too long, the suffering of the world had locked him inside this prison, and a resurgence of love was his only hope. There was no joy in his voice, nor a suggestion of a smile, like he was so attached to the place I lived in for ten years, to the failures I had, to the land where I once planned to commit suicide in, a land that witnessed all my personality changes. He was not used to the new me.

"You're making me weak," he said, right before his voice faded, slow and steady.

Everyone says he is not real, that a knock on the head can do strange things to a person, but I know what I hear. His voice is clear, and his tone has softened as he urged me to stay with him.

They say that the marks on your heart tell you where you're going, but the marks on your face tell you where you've been.

"Khaled, you're a fighter."

A phrase that I heard a lot from many people I met throughout my journey. But am I really?

I went to wake up Marina so we don't get late on our flight. We took a cab and headed to the airport.

The airport looked more like a shopping mall. The tiles under foot gleamed white, and everywhere were people milling around, moving as chaotic rainbows, colors so brilliant. They flowed from the check-in desks to the cafes and through the gates, each one of them heading for a destination of their own making. There were two glass elevators leading to an upper floor which had the appearance of a food mall. And in the middle of several large open areas were blue fabric-covered seats. The air was cool, and only the faint aroma coming down from the food area gave it any scent. Some stairs lead up to a viewing deck where eager children watched the airplanes take off and land. As Adam and Nour dashed toward the mounted telescopes that were there to look through, the back wall was one large window and behind the telescopes was a scale model of the airport with the runways marked on it.

Who knew my journey would end soon? I walked with my luggage checking my passport once or twice. The steps that I took forward on those sleek silvery tiles of the airport terminal were trembling, but I knew I had to move forward, leaving behind all the memories that had been attached to me. All those around had their inner emotion portrayed on their faces.

No matter how salubrious the furnishings inside the airplane were, to Marina, it would never be more than a flying metal tube. She recited her prayer as she stepped over the threshold and smiled stiffly at the stewardess.

I was told to sit in row fifteen, chair twenty-six, with my family on either side of me. As the wing sliced through the clouds, I tried to see the remaining fragments. Clouds pooled around the great mountains, slightly changing from pearl white to calm yellow, warmly glowing in the summer sunshine.

I laid eyes on my homeland Egypt once again.

Chapter 12
Faith

I am walking in a long corridor of an empty hospital, the hallway has as much personality as the rest of the hospital. The floor is slate grey, and the walls dove. Above the ceiling is made from those polystyrene squares laid on a grid-like frame, it's clear and high arched, it's like standing out in the open without the risk of rain, the light is too bright for my eyes after the darkening gloom outside, I find it abrasive, enough perhaps to bring on one of my migraines. There are commercial prints on the wall, tasteful in the dull kind of way.

Multiple rooms on both sides, above every door I pass, is a large plastic sign, dark with white lettering, no fancy fonts, just bold and all-caps. It's so new and spotless I feel like the whole building must have just gotten beamed here from someplace dirt is outlawed.

The air had a pure fragrance, not sterile, just clean. In the background played music at just the right level to give the patients an emotional lift, I keep on hearing these loud radio noise from one of the rooms, and I keep following the sounds, that same radio channel my mother used to turn on when she used to wake us up for school, as soon as I finally find the radio, I lower the volume, and keep moving forward in the hallway. Something is drawing me until I saw my father in one of the rooms.

Paralyzed I became for some fragments of moments, I hugged him while tears kept on drooping on his shoulders. I miss that hug, I had a lot to tell him after he walked away, yet we are silent.

"Nour is here too," Dad said.

I beg him to see her while mom is pulling me away, wanting to take me home, but I insist.

We reach her room. Oh girl, she's sleeping her little angelic sleep, she's sleeping on her left arm, and her hand wasn't visible.

Shocked again I was, as she turns to me and I couldn't believe my eyes, she had no left arm. I look at my father who started explaining to me what happened, but all I remember is that he told me.

"Although she has one arm, I'll raise her very well, she has a promising future."

Nour starts to open her eyes, she wakes up, and she spells my name just like she used to spell it in the past. I hold her close, my grip is so tight, I refuse to let her go, and with an eye full of tears. I tell her I miss her.

It was a cold March night when I woke up to that cryptic dream, a dream maybe until now I didn't arrive to comprehend, but I woke up with a feeling of relief after seeing their faces one more time.

And so, I am back in Egypt! Welcome to the jungle, where everyone is climbing on one another to reach their goal and to write their own success story, hospitals choose who and what best suits them and draws the best financial gain, a jungle where doctors are being recruited in top hospitals mostly for their contacts, a family relative or perhaps a mutual benefit, rather than their knowledge and years of studying and commitment. It's only money that speaks out here in the real world.

I walked up to my homedoor, dragging my luggage behind me. I raised my hand to knock, but I stopped. I took a deep breath and forced myself to hit the door bell. I heard the "ding-dong" sound coming from inside and someone running to get the door.

It opened slowly, and my mother's warm, loving face was revealed. I embraced her in a tight hug, suddenly unsure why I hadn't returned in so long.

It was strange being home again after so long. Despite how long I'd been away, I still remembered everything about this place; the blue hydrangeas planted in the front yard, the soft tinkling of the wind chimes that reminded me of summer afternoons. The blue paint had faded since I had last seen it, but I still recognized it. It looked like the color of the sky before a bad storm.

After a handful of ten fat years abroad, Streets were different; people looked different, even my home was different. I left this place when I was a non-social creature filled with insecurities, a boy whom his heart skips a beat when the home phone rings, who avoided answering the phone to not reveal his stutter to strangers. An addict, and a teenager who couldn't care less what his future holds for him as long as he stays hidden from the world behind his computer screen, and no one knows about his stutter, so afraid of being exposed.

It's definitely a different feeling when you come back to a place where you once felt so weak even to stand for your own self and take a look at it from a new life perspective. I am wiser, bigger, braver, and more sanguine now.

I've lived my life until this moment like a backpacker, changing places, changing homes all the time. I was deprived of stability, these changes led to many consequences, positive and negative, it definitely accentuated my character, but on the other hand, it was a reason enough to cut all my relations with any friends I ever had, even my best friends were forgotten by time, they say time kills everything that's bad, unfortunately, it also kills anything that's good.

I had to start from scratch again in Egypt, we lived with a limited income, Adam and Nour going to kindergarten, my wife always complaining about how difficult her life is here, I was always democratic with her, having the ability to turn her mood upside down and the intelligence to turn a heated conversation to jokes and laughs and a kiss on the forehead, that was just me.

My old friends, their faces have quiet changed, their life paths were diverse, even their jokes were different, some of them got married, some fell in love, and some lost the love of their lives, some earned a life-changing job, and some were drowning in debts, some were just celebrating the birth of their kids, and some parted from our world whom I regret that I never got to see their faces again.

It took quite a while till I was able to rebuild that bond with them again, till I was able to synchronize myself with any group of friends I get out with. It took a while till they got used to my stuttering again.

My mother was helping financially until I find a job, but it wasn't that easy. I was searching everywhere, until one day I had an unpleasant conversation with my mother while eating dinner on the table.

"Khaled, don't get used to this money. You're the most spoilt and careless out of my sons."

Now hearing these words as a big boy with two kids and a wife on his shoulders wasn't really the best thing to hear, but I was raised in a way to never hold anger on the ones who raised me, especially my mother. That time I couldn't hold it. While I fully understand her point telling me these words, she shouldn't have said it in such a way whatsoever.

I felt offended, I just stood up of the dinner table and left, indignant that even the closest people sometimes can't relate to how hard you're trying. I went back home, sat between the arms of my wife, narrating to her what happened as she was understanding. I just needed someone to unload to.

Not much time after I returned to Egypt, my younger brother was graduating from his university, finishing his army, and receiving his first work contract abroad where he had to leave, going to South Africa.

My story with Muhammad, my younger brother, has always been incomplete. Our existence was never for long in the same place. However, he was always proud of what am doing in my life, even at times I was a loser, he never stopped supporting me even for one day, throughout the time I missed all of his teenage years when I was in Ukraine, sometimes I wish I was with him to teach him some of the things I learned, but I never got the chance to leave a mark on him as an older brother, as our father is gone, I am sure he always had a lot of questions as a teenager that demanded to be answered, am also sure that Karim was always there for him as a brother and a father.

Muhammad is a big man now, but he never shows that in front of me. He's rather always hungry to hear and listen attentively to all what I've been through.

While always remembering how he was crying when I stayed at home alone with him and Karim on the day of the accident and how I took him between my arms to calm him down, he left to South Africa for a long-term contract, but he always came back in vacations, all gifted-up to all of the family, he's the best uncle my kids can ever have.

Days and months passed by while still on an active search for a job as a doctor, a living to sustain my family's future. I had to find myself a day-to-day job between a taxi driver and a waiter just to keep some bread on the table for my family while parallelly doing numerous interviews.

I was twenty-eight when I saw my first prestigious dream job. I thought back then that I'd just apply, and they'll accept me, sigh! If only it was that easy; it was my first job interview in a reputable clinic in town; everything was going as planned.

My shift as a waiter at the pizza parlor had overrun, and now I was late for my hospital interview. I ran down the crowded street, dodging shoppers and office workers on their way home. How I longed to be headed home too, or even better, to have a job that paid enough to order in pizza or buy fancy coffee instead of using my pot of Nescafe. My stomach growled, but there was no time to eat now. I stopped running just before the glass front of the hospital, smoothed my hair down, rearranged my face into an expression I hopped, looked relaxed and happy, and strolled in through those automatic doors.

There was no back wall to the interview room, only tempered glass. I was expecting it to appear blackened as it did from the outside, yet it was crystal clear with the most stunning panorama of the city, the trees below like the ones on my son's miniature train table. I tried to smile, but a twitch was all I managed as I focused on the four people at the table, blue and shinier than a summertime lake. Each one of them looked my way just as friendly as a kindly relative, yet still, my insides contracted like the air were an arctic flow.

"We'll be calling you soon," they said.

Days and weeks passed by, waiting desperately for their answer. I knew after that they have hired someone else.

My first job rejection was so hard to swallow, but it made me never stop wondering, why? If everything was going very well in the interview, I answered all the questions. What is the reason for rejection after all? Especially that it happened with many following jobs after that, it usually happened with an almost typical scenario.

Employers never wanted to confront me. Perhaps they were shy to tell me they don't want to hire a stutterer, that's all I really wanted to hear after all, rather than wondering and doubting myself and although being full of myself in every interview I make, I was sure that I have all the qualities to fit in the vacancies I applied for.

As much as it seemed like a harsh thing to say but I truly wanted to hear it to my face, for all I want is to cut all the doubts. However, I never did. Not a single interviewer had the guts to confront me with the real problem of why I get rejected.

I was mad like an angry bull who's full of enthusiasm, excitement, and passion for functioning impeccably in every spot I applied to; however, I couldn't care less. Yes, it's true that I desperately needed every job and vacancy I applied for, but with every rejection, I always had a feeling that someone up there had a better plan for me. It's called Faith.

Chapter 13
The Crippled

"Happy birthday to you"
"Happy birthday to you"
"Happy birthday to daddy"
"Happy birthday to you."

It's the first day of my thirties and I wake up on a lovely chant and a cake from my wife and kids. It is moments like these that always remind you of God's blessings and keeps you on track for whatever hunt and goal you're after.

At this age, a birthday is a quiet day. It is a day to reflect on the year that was and what is ahead to strive for. I guess it is a sort of personal "New Year"; one where resolutions can be made, promises to the self. For me, I plan to be bolder, to speak louder about the ideas I have for making a better world for all lives on earth. Perhaps that extra bit of bravery, that extra bit of willpower and resolve, is the real gift to myself from me. This time next year I will be a better and a more confident person, then make another resolution the year after.

I kissed them warmly and decided to take them on a two hours road trip to spend a couple of days by the beach.

Adam was growing so fast before my bare eyes, his character was getting formed, and I got so emotionally connected to him by the time he was three.

As I watch him build a castle and as sand slides from the bucket. For that tiny moment, the waves hush, and the birds hold their chattering. I feel as if the beach is a photograph, and I am eternal within it. I dream of the inner life of his castle, the one formed at his touch. Music bounces from within, notes dancing, bringing the people to movement. I saw a million sunrises and the starry nights that follow, each as crisp and perfect as the last. And then the moment blossoms into a fresh one.

The corner of the castle crumbles as if it were a raisin cake at the hand of a hungry child. Adam laughs. Now the sandcastle has character, it is free of the walls that made it, no chains, breathing in the seaside air. I picked him up and threw him up high just like my father used to.

As he reached the age of six, I noticed something is changing in his speaking pattern, not like before, some interruptions, it took me a while to confirm, or perhaps to convince myself that he's experiencing stuttering.

Loving him was blind. I didn't want my over-care to spoil everything, where in fact, I was dying inside, picturing all my life experiences, what I've been and still going through. I didn't want him to go through all of that.

I was reading more and more about stuttering inheritance.

"Developmental stuttering may run in families. In 2010, for the first time, NIDCD researchers isolated three genes that cause stuttering."

A phrase from an article that I read at the time, even though it was confirmed that it could be inherited, at the same time, too many studies were showing that it has nothing to do with family history.

I was sleepless for days.

I decided not to repeat the same mistake my parents once made, focusing the spotlights on my stutter and making a big deal out of it. Love can come in different ways; over-worrying can lead to the exact thing you keep worrying about. As much as it was hard for me to swallow, I forced myself to play blind while he's talking with me, not giving it the slightest attention, watching him from far away. How is he reacting with his sister, with his friends? Is it bothering him? In which letters does he stutter the most, and what are the most difficult words for him? Is he forcing the words to come out?

Astonishingly, I realized that he himself wasn't even aware of his stutter.

Just like all the kids all over the world, we waved goodbye to his stutter, which persisted for around two months, and then parted away and never came back.

As I remember a quote I once read by Paulo Coelha saying, *"The more attention you pay an enemy, the stronger you make him. Be attentive, but don't be paranoiac."* It all then came into play.

Throughout the years, my mother's love to my kids went far beyond her love to me, that grandmother-love was real, although she could so easily assume a stern and commanding air, it was by no means habitual to her; and the children, though they feared and never dared to dispute her authority, soon loved her with all the pure, unselfish love of childhood, which cannot be bought. The kids loved spending time with her while she narrates many life stories and teaches them their religion.

On the other hand, my mother was still struggling in courts to get our inheritance rights from my father's business partner, who recently lost his daughter in a typical car accident, I've never seen karma hit back that fierce, but well, sometimes it does.

After almost twelve years of a running case in tribunals, on a Monday morning, it was made clear the judge's last and final call for our litigation, a call that is no more appealable, a case that we lost.

Following that, my mother was passing through a period of recession, always thinking about all the effort done through all these years, all for nothing.

My brothers and I stayed next to her in these times to cheer her up.

"It's not the end of the world, mom, we'll live through this, and we'll make you proud," I told her in a long night after a dinner out.

Sometimes even after a long pursuit, we don't get what we want. There is always a time for everything.

And so, back to me, within a couple of months from residing in Egypt, I got myself hooked up in a football team, my shining was relatively faster than I expected in the football community here. I was chosen to represent the country in their national team; people viewed me as a leader; despite my stuttering, I still had my own insecurities that had to be secretly dealt with.

It was then when I acknowledged that some people actually do pay attention to the talents and skills you show rather than how you talk or even what you talk. The level of professionalism and your results could speak for theirselves.

It wasn't long till I was asked to coach young athletes, full of enthusiasm, passion for the game, and the urge to get better. I promised myself before committing to them; to teach them every single thing I know, everything I learned, outside the field before inside about losing battles and winning wars, about picking yourself up after getting beaten to death, and about never losing hope even if it looks unattainable.

Through the years, I started as a coaching assistant, moved to a position coach, then to a defensive coordinator, and all the way to a head coach. I was feeling so powerful from the inside, but at the same time, I was humble and always counted God's blessings.

I was nominated for a head coach position to a women's football club, a team of more than forty young girls and ex-champions of their current league.

I was loaded with doubts. After all, it's a position that demanded a very high level of charisma, a leadership level I wasn't even sure I am on, despite everyone else seeing it in me. My stuttering wasn't always making me feel full of myself. Taurus wasn't.

After deciding to not just give it a try but to rather prove myself even more in the football community, I accepted the proposal, and on the first day of practice, I gathered the girls and introduced myself.

"HHHello girls, I am KhKhaled Bassyouny, your new hhhhead coach and a football veteran, and I ssstutter just in case you're wondering. I am nnnot only your coach, am yyyyour ffffriend too and I am only hhhere to help you aaachieve your aaathletic goals, you'll ppprobably love me and hate me at the same time but it's all for your own good. Ladies, iiit's my pleasure cccoaching you this season."

Publicly acknowledging my stutter once again, just like I did in my university presentation, it was working.

I started using my new technique everywhere I go, in any awkward situation as well as with new people when I feel that I'll start to lose it. It was my secret recipe to remove the tension from any speech.

And so, exposing my stuttering was a vital key in my journey of attaining fluency.

By that time, it became a ritual. I used to make motivational speeches on the team. My team reached the bowl that year. I would say I was a successful coach.

In addition to that, sometimes, when stuttering got really nasty, I started to make fun out of it, which was even more powerful.

In other words, it was magical. I learned to make a fool out of Taurus; everywhere I go, it seemed like I knew everything about him. Maybe at times, he seemed so vulnerable to me. I wanted him to stay silent forever.

It was at these times when I learned that *one proves that he's confident and full of himself only when he's able to make fun of his own insecurities openly.*

One evening post practice, one of my players invited me to her wedding party which was going to take a place in a week. And so, I got all tuxed up, looking glamorous and fresh that evening, stepping my foot in the hall, there were many people I know, old friends and new friends, young men and women of my age.

It was that moment when the bridesmaids rushed forward and began struggling for the slippers, to the damage and disarray of their gowns, and when they were halfway up, the bride heaved the bouquet, and it burst apart among them like a bomb of colored fragrance, and the girls below snatched at the flowers, shrieking deliriously.

The place was super crowded; everyone was doing the thing they do best, socializing, speaking, and just making new friends, while me, being in atmospheres like these, always tend to wake Taurus up, letting him loose trying to get a hold of me. I thought that my game with women was done after five years of marriage. I thought that I couldn't open any topic confidently or even spark attraction with any woman if I want to.

Then the music became as loud as thunder. It made the cutlery on the tabletops rattle. Neon lights flashed everywhere like police sirens, but much more colorful.

Meanwhile, while being there lurking in my inner thoughts, a young lady approached me.

"You must be the Hellhounds linebacker they're talking about," she said.

"That's true. I am that hot guy the city kkkeeps talking about. Do you want an autograph?" I replied sarcastically. We exchanged some good laughs and had a long talk that night. My conversation was fluent to the extent that I couldn't believe am not stuttering. Neither did anyone notice that from the people I spoke with that night.

While the girl was apparently into me, she couldn't hide it, and while she was attempting to get to know me more, I had to excuse myself that night to get back to my wife and kids, whom I was really missing.

And in case you're wondering, yes, I've always been that type of man, loyalty always comes with a price.

Days passed by, and I was still unemployed in the medical field. My financial level was getting lower and lower. I spent all the money of my father's fortune on my ten years of studies; payback time was due. I finally got employed in a faraway peripheral hospital, so far from home, I used to travel twelve hours by train, a week on week off from my house.

Being away for long times was always a reason for increasing tensions between me and my wife.

On the other side of the coin, Nour was growing up faster than I could handle; parenting a baby girl was different than I ever imagined, she was very sensitive to my feelings, and she sensed every mood swing I had, even before she could talk, she was watching everything I do. If I cut my hair, she would cry; if I got new pair of shoes, she would wear them, she started speaking earlier than her brother, she was looking for ways to communicate with me, and once she started to form sentences and be able to actually talk, she turned into a chatterbox narrating her whole day to me, she started to have opinions about her outfit, lots of opinions, she would instantly take off what her mom puts on her if she doesn't like it. But it was always fun to watch her dress herself. I also learned that not all girls love pink.

Until one day, by the time she was five, I saw her laugh when I asked her something while stuttering.

"Daddy, why do you talk like that?" she asked.

"Baby girl, every one of us got his own superpower that makes him stronger and different than others, just like superheroes."

"Wow, so this is your superpower! Daddy, what is my superpower?"

"It's your tongue, baby, you speak a lot!"

Nour was and will always remain a blessing to my life.

On the same side, Adam was maturing. He used to see me and his mother fight over the tiniest things. While I always try to take him away from our fights and tell him to close the door when we're arguing loudly, he always insisted on entering and standing between us, in hope to make things better, expecting us to stop arguing, but sometimes we just didn't, every so often his kid instinct used to tell him to push his sister to stand between us when he notices that we're still too attached to the argument that we're not paying attention to him anymore.

Yes, It's sad. We don't get to choose what memories get engraved in the brains of our children and what doesn't. They just retain the memories that made an impact on them at some point in their lives, makes me sit and just hope that the times where he got to witness these arguments and fights don't affect him someday in the future.

On long train journeys to the hospital, sometimes there was no place on the train, but I had to get on it anyway, stay in the train corridor for the whole twelve hours, sometimes even sleeping on its floor hallway just to arrive at work on time.

It was moments like these that made me cherish how I lived when I was a student, made me think about the times I used to squander money relentlessly hanging out, going to parties, and buying useless stuff. Things are a little different now. Having a family is totally unalike. It's that sense of responsibility that makes you try to save every penny to keep some bread on the table, something only true men would relate to.

I was in continuous promotions until I reached a position of a resident in the specialty that is most close to my heart, plastic surgery.

After one and a half years, I got relocated to a hospital that is near my home, more specialized in General surgery. I barely slept, stuck between night shifts, daytime clinics, and emergency rooms 24/7. I gained my charisma so fast in that place, my skills in surgery were increasing day by day, my boss used to designate me interns to mentor them, boys and girls, enthusiasts to learn more about medicine, I made sure I teach them everything I know.

It was a period where I almost spent all national holidays and weekends in the hospital. I even celebrated New Year with my patients and the nursing staff. I was always informed that doctors never get to live like other people, but I never thought to this extent, it's never a nine to five job, or at least it was not for this period of my career, as much as I was getting exhausted, perhaps sometimes disappointed I don't spend times with my family like before, but I was happy I am improving day by day, and finally practicing what I was urging to do for a very long time.

Time was flying, I used to experience severe abdominal aches periodically that I usually ignored it to my always busy schedule, until I was diagnosed with an intestinal disease that needed to be operated on, I knew I had it for a long time, but I was always so involved in my work, family, and football that I almost didn't have the time to take this seriously. every time I would postpone the operation especially that it was no emergency, until one day, I started bleeding.

After all, and as a doctor, I didn't practice what I preach. It was the typical price you pay for being ignorant and careless about your welfare.

The blood didn't gush in a constant flow, but in time with the beating of my heart. At first, it came thick and strong, flowing through my fingers as I feel my pulse. I felt the blood move over my hand, the thick fluid no warmer or cooler than my own skin. After a few moments more the blood was still leaving my rapidly paling flesh, but the pulses were slower, weaker; until I had to undergo immediate surgery.

It made me wonder about my job a little bit. Although I do my job as a surgeon. I never really understood that patients are so helpless. I never really looked at the whole hospital/operation room experience from the eyes of a patient. Luckily, I am honored to have gone through this.

Wearing the operation coat on a naked body in a very cold theatre, that pain of a cannula insertion, cold liquid running through my veins, my first spinal puncture, and feeling the numbness slowly spreading through my legs. Laying down on the operation bed having to stare at the ceiling for two hours, getting driven to my room on my bed passing by the whole surgery department where I once walked and controlled everything there, only it's the other way around now, I am that helpless patient that's in deep need of the care of roaming nurses.

I start re-gaining back my sensations, I could feel it one cell at a time. What is the real meaning of urinary retention, no really, that pain, and how miraculous a catheter can be. I got to know how strong and potent pain killers can unquestionably matter.

As we grow older, we grow wiser, and we start to cherish those tiny details we once took for granted, one of which is surely being in good health.

I am glad I got to see the world from a different perspective. I can already see it reflecting on me.

On my return back home after being discharged from the hospital, Marina was there for me all the time, the least to say that getting off painkillers and starting to continue my life without them wouldn't have been easier if she wasn't by my side.

Half a year in, I welcomed a new group of sixth-year medical students who was happening to do two months round in surgery under my command, I saw that new student. His face looked familiar, but I would never be able to remember where I saw it, those dark eyes, that laugh, and that scar over his left eyebrow.

Day in day out, when I used to explain things to the students, he wouldn't look at my face. He never did.

Until that time when I was having a quick snack between two stressful operations, I was assisting in, enjoying five minutes of calmness sipping on my coffee cup held tightly by my right-hand fingers, while parallelly biting on a butter and honey toast with my left hand, lurking in a quiet state of mind, trying not to stress just about anything.

He knocked on the door and asked if he can come in.

"Hello, doc."

"Hey, Amr, hhhow are you? Do yyyou need something?"

"I wanted to ask if I can assist you in the next operation."

I looked at him and answered, "No."

following an awkward silence, I smiled and said, "Nnnot before you tell me wwwhere did we meet before."

"You don't remember?"

"No, I don't."

"We were classmates in primary school, but I was never your friend. You probably hated me."

I flashed back for a moment.

I went back to where it all happened, watching all my childhood memories being replayed in front of my mere eyes like a tape put on fast-forward, kids laughing at me, mimicking my speech and my tone, calling me "The crippled."

"I am the crippled," I said.

Chapter 14
Un-Chained

Fires of fury and hatred were smoldering in my small, narrowed eyes as I weighed the pros and cons of the various and creative means available to me for exacting revenge.

The anger from my eyes showed the scared child within. It boiled deep in my system, as hot as lava. It churned within, hungry for destruction, and I know it's too much for me to handle. The pressure of this raging sea of anger would force me to say things I do not mean or to express thoughts I've suppressed for years.

I know I have to get out of everyone's way before I erupt in my furious state. I know that this feeling will pass, but while it hasn't, I'm well aware I could really hurt people.

Taurus awakened all of a sudden, telling me to smack the crap out of him right now, but as I took a deep breath, I've managed to contain my outrage.

It was then when I learned that, anytime that old devil gets in my head, always on about the hating and the entitlements, the blame game, and the shame, I simply hang up the phone. I've got too much of God's work to do, too much loving and helping. Who's got time for all that when there are so many in need and so much to be thankful for?

My hatred started melting, and I slowly emerged from the anger I possessed. Having the anger dissipate in me felt nice, and I felt calmer than I had before. I felt free.

"I am sorry, I was young and stupid. Forgive me," he told me with a face full of regret.

"You're right, I did hate you at that time, but I would like to thank you, you played a role in putting me where I am today. If your guilt tears at your heart, rips at your insides, you are already forgiven," I said with an open, clear heart, literally not carrying a single gram of grudge.

Sometimes, if a bad memory is like a bird, it is okay to know it is sitting on a branch nearby. It is okay to notice it fly and sing. Yet move in calmness with eyes only for the nature around you, with skin that feels the wind and eyes that open for the light. When your mind naturally moves back into the present, into the moment that is the gift of life, the bird will be gone.

Even after eighteen years, I thought about him every now and then; however, in our lives, we meet people. Some we never think about again. Some, we wonder what happened to them. There are some that we wonder if they ever think about us. And then there are some we wish we never had to think about again. But we do.

Sometimes it's hard to forgive such acts from persons that caused you lifetime scars, but if you look deeper at these scars, you'll love them, you'll love how they formed you, built you from the inside, as they sure didn't kill you but definitely got you stronger.

We then had a long gossip, shared some memories of our childhood. He told me about how things changed since I left the school and how all the class heard about the tragedy that happened to my family. He confessed that my chair and desk in the class were always missed.

It felt good to reminisce not all but enough old memories to make us bond again.

"You still look like a pig, though." I told him sarcastically.

We shared a few laughs before I ordered him to get sterilized for our next operation as we ran out of time.

He was overwhelmed. Since then, he became my best student.

Even then, when my confidence levels were relatively high, it still wasn't easy. I still stuttered on some occasions, there were times when I thought I got a hand of it. I was always experimenting, trying different things I invented to use when a block comes to my speech, I attempted disengaging myself and thinking of something else, or substitute the word with another one conveying the same meaning, and everytime when I think I understand everything about it and how to control it, I come to the conclusion that I always fail to solve this riddle, I know absolutely nothing, the stutter was very rational, it came at times I didn't even expect, and was absent at times where I expected it to jump in, trying to understand stuttering and how can you make it stop, for me it was pretty much similar like that myth of trying to understand women.

I remember on a December night-shift in the hospital, I was chatting with a patient, taking notes of his medical history while his family was with him, when all of a sudden, I started stuttering, they obviously were trying to contain a laughter they longed to let go throughout my conversation with him, while me remaining so calm from the inside.

It made me wonder how and why I was so calm. While being in a position of power and authority like that, I could've easily kicked them out of the room, but that wouldn't have helped either. I couldn't remember when was the last time I got this kind of reaction, probably years ago. Life taught me to always be calm in these situations.

I walked out of the patient's room proudly like nothing ever happened. As a matter of fact, nothing really did happen. It was just the reaction of some people who probably never saw a stutterer in their lives. I don't blame them for their ignorance either, for later on, they were thanking me for treating their son.

As I age, people's reactions were and still the last thing I think about if I happen to stutter, the reactions I reap had always been a factor trying hard to get into my emotions, but I am not that fourteen years old anymore.

Speaking of emotions, there was still that one thing that never failed to touch my emotions, so deep that it's actually able to touch my stomach.

A shawarma!

Regardless of my age, grabbing one every now and then was always a lifetime hobby. My little ones were loving it as well. I developed a habit of telling them a new thing about their great grandfather every time we sit for a shawarma, how successful he was, how he started from scratch, how he cared for my mother, and how strong his love was for me.

And so, the time finally came to take my career to a different level.

"Khaled, I want you to present this case in our next meeting," said my boss.

I didn't even think twice before I found myself saying, "SSSorry sir, but I would not be able to do that, pppplease put any other doctor in my place this time."

"Are you sure, Khaled?"

"Yes, sir."

Facing my phobia is not as easy as it seems, an undeniable fear of presentations or public speaking in general, a fear developed throughout the years and enriched by my previous experiences that just the thought of me standing on stage alone talking to the public was enough to amplify my heart rate to the double. A terrifying monster, a red line I was ought not to cross, and crossing it just seemed absurd.

Throwing back my memories of my first day in school or the day of presenting my master's degree, or even ordering food in restaurants. Many occasions where I just failed myself, and too many failures and disappointments to count that made me repeat all the time the phrase.

"I hate public speaking."

My boss decided to give the opportunity to another doctor.

I was there when my colleague was offered this chance.

I was there when she jumped out of her chair from joy. I was there among the audience when she was speaking on stage, and the entire crowd applauded for her.

And I was also there when she got her promotion due to this presentation a couple of weeks after that. I was truly happy for her and truly confused about myself.

This fear is my challenge and my demon to slay, for it will come until I do, unannounced and gnarly. The only way out is to order this brain to function, to demand solutions instead of this crazy-making circling anxiety. So though it feels as if my bones have no more strength and my muscles are all out of power, I still have the option to remain still, to be quiet enough to choose how to fight.

Meanwhile, I was still applying to different better hospitals for a chance to step up my career, always trying to climb up that ladder until I actually got accepted in a part-time job in one of the main city hospitals in the capital, Cairo.

I remember I was overjoyed. I walked around spreading my happiness to my friends and close ones, having this vision of my financial level who will finally be a little higher, my kids will get in better schools, and I would be able to finally buy my wife a small gift of appreciation, a tribute of her long journey with me.

My shifts in the new hospital were supposed to start in two weeks. I got myself a new scrub and stethoscope. I kept studying even more than before to get ready to cope with the new genre of patients frequenting that hospital.

As the lines of glares that shot for my eyelids awakened me, my first morning I woke up to my new work, hoping for a smooth and pleasant day, I dressed up and left my house while my wife and kids are sleeping. You'd think the road would be empty at six in the morning. Everyone should be asleep, right? Maybe except a few doctors and nurses, those wonderful folks the world can't turn without.

My car joins a train of others, mostly other office works with "vital" paper to push for twelve or more hours. In summer, there is daylight, not so much for the rest of the year. I follow the red tail lights. This morning the sky has an unusual dash of orange cast onto the otherwise pale grey cloud. Otherwise, the day promises to be like every other. The road is washed black by recent rain, and the sidewalks are almost empty. As my car hits the street, my mind moves rapidly to autopilot mode, and as soon as I entered the hospital in the early morning.

"Dr. Khaled, the medical director of the hospital, would like to speak with you," said the girl in the reception office.

"Sure, let me just put my scrubs on and go to his office." We had a long conversation. It was like a whole new interview until I was asked to leave the job for another doctor, who's more qualified, as they said.

I got rejected on my first day of a new job, for forever to be an anonymous reason, at least for me it was, who would ever reject someone after already accepting him? How humiliating would that be?

Next thing I know I was losing my nerves.

Every word stung, only fueling the fire that burned inside of me. Every violated phrase was like gasoline to it.

I swallowed that anger when it was a fire-seed and forgot to drink something cool, and so it grew in my belly until it came out as hot as any dragon has ever flamed, my fists began to clench, and my jaw rooted. When the final mento had been added to the coke inside of me, I exploded with anger, with no control, objects levitated and broke. People dropped to the floor as the primeval instinct took over.

"Tell me the reason, tell me the goddamn reason, why are you refusing me after I already got accepted? Do you think it's a game? Am I not good-looking enough? Am I dumb? Do I stink? Maybe I am too nice? Too polite? Or does my social standard doesn't fit with your hospital? or perhaps is it because I STUTTER? tell me."

"Dr. Khaled, I think it's better for you to leave now."

It's been there a while now, this anger, escaping when I'm away from those I love. I'm angry at store clerks and car drivers. Heck, I'm even angry if my sandwich isn't quite right.

The truth is, my life needs to change for the better because there's more going into this brain and body than I can handle and still be me. So, even if it's not okay, I'm going to start working on my real dreams.

And so, I looked at him pathetically and left the room.

Since then, I never knew why I got rejected again; some days I hope that he just had the guts to tell me, "yes, it's because of your stutter." I needed to hear this killing answer, an answer that would fuel me up to push harder, that's me. But he never said it and left me drowning in a sea of question marks and self-doubts, a conundrum of an ocean of thoughts in my head.

I shed a couple of tears on my way out, got myself back up, and drove to the hospital I was working in as I had to work there at night.

I came back home the next morning tired after a long night shift, by returning home, I feel like a tortoise retracting into her shell. The troubles of the world are evaporating. To everyone else, this is a house like all the other houses on this street, but to me, it is a sanctuary. It is a cocoon. It is rest.

Serving myself a cup of coffee, sitting alone in my 14th story balcony, looking at people from up there, watching them as they chatter about anything and everything.

Although I can't hear what they talk about, I could always see they're enjoying it.

In a world full of technology and social media, talking will forever remain a blessing, a gift everyone should enjoy and never take for granted. Being able to communicate verbally, being heard, and answered to is priceless.

While I sip on my coffee, I tend to keep thinking about the presentation I passed on to my colleague, leading to her promotion.

"What are you waiting for?" said Taurus.

"Am not ready."

"You'll never know you're ready or not if you don't try."

"I tried several times before. I was a joke."

"That was the old you, the Khaled I used to own, a Khaled who was so subliminal to my commands, now I have no power on you. You're stronger than I expected you to be, stronger than anyone expected you to be. You've reached so many successes at a young age, and you still think about your stutter when it should be the last thing in your mind by now. You've opened new horizons and set foot in places you yourself didn't think you would see, It was all you, not me. Khaled, our differences and imperfections makes us humans, don't try to hide something that makes you unique, accept it, and so will others. You should be proud of yourself, because I am of you."

That day, that breezy day, I let his voice soak in, his words. I had a smile on my face, a different kind of smile. That's when my wife entered, hugged me from my back, and asked me what's making me smile.

This is the confidence of the phoenix, of one who has suffered into ash, reborn in the flames of hot pain and commanded to sing. This is confidence hard-won yet deep, anchored in the true self that is always safe at my core. It is that which grows in within, purging that which was born of fear, clearing the way for love to grow, to take up every aspect of who I am. And in this rawness, in this absolute vulnerability, I am confident because, in these words, I found myself.

I resonated my mind with my soul and welcomed Taurus back. Like an old friend coming back from a very long journey, he innervated me the confidence I needed like he used to do when I was a child, and I became at peace with myself and who I am.

The next morning sun shined so fast, I woke up, brushed my teeth, and went to work. The first thing I did is that I asked my boss if I can get an opportunity to present a big case I've been working on. He took off his glasses, looked straight into my eyes, and paused for a couple of seconds.

"Sure," he answered.

He double-checked for the availability of all the doctors in the hospital, of different fields and specialties, starting from the head of departments all the way to interns. He got back to me two days later with a confirmed date. He made sure I had a vast audience this time.

And so, the next Sunday arrived, it was a windy dawn, my alarm rang at 5:00, I've been waiting for this morning for so long that I barely believe my eyes when the sharp shadows cast by the street-lamps through my metallic blinds start to fade, diluted by the onset of daylight. Then a chorus of birds breaks the drone of the city traffic. I know it's too early to be up, but I've waited for this day for so long. I've trained for it for twelve long years, and now it's here.

I woke up to the usual sounds of the trains near my home; everybody's rushing to work, the morning is as assured as the tides and just as unstoppable. I need a few more hours of blackness. Not to sleep, but to prepare, to pour my thoughts out onto a page, reorganize, prioritize and pack them back in again. Soon there will be color and traffic noises, the smell of other residents making coffee and toast. Today I break free. Today there is a plan, and I can't afford to mess it up. My script lies cold at the foot of the thin blanket, not feeling the weight of destiny or the immense burden of my expectations. It has taken so long to craft. I wake up and sit on the bed for a few minutes before I get up to take a shower.

I do my prayers, kiss my kids and wife goodbye, and take my car all the way to work. While I refrain from being distracted, my side vision is almost blurred. I can already see myself dominating the stage, killing the presentation, and answering every question. I can already see my confident self-up there finishing my last word and nailing a big round of applause from the entire hall.

I step foot into the presentation hall, the ceiling must be twenty feet high. Designs of fruit and flowers are carved into the molding, and small, fat children with wings look down at us from every angle. Vases of blossoms give off a cloying scent that makes my eyes itch.

I am finally there, along with two other presenters before me. The room includes more than one hundred doctors. I go to take a seat, then here comes my favorite game of turns, but today, it's running so fast that I don't even remember panicking, as a matter of fact, I can't wait for my turn to come, I can't wait to go out there and just, speak.

It wasn't long until I found myself up there. After stepping on stage, I had an awkward silence for a few seconds. I was scanning the auditorium. So many myriads of faces like beads on a bead-work pattern, all bead-work, in different layers, I can see the crowd, I wasn't hiding my eyes, neither was my vision blurry, I was looking at every single one of the audiences in the eye, I embraced my stutter and said,

"Ladies and GGentlmen, I am KhKhaled Bassyouny, the stuttering doctor you heard about…"

Now there could be an audience of a million strong. I would be okay with that because the only person's opinion I cared for was myself. So regardless of the glare of the lights or the expanse of the stage, I was always right there in that first moment I rose on the stage. I could stand up and speak to anyone, anywhere in the world, and it would be the same as sitting on my couch at home.

Following quiet a long presentation that went flawlessly, the interaction from the crowd was remarkable, numerous questions being asked while being able to hold the conversation at the level I always wanted it to be.

With the cheers come hands in the air and eyes flung wide. Twenty-five minutes through, the cheers erupt like an auditory volcano. It is all quiet one second and then deafening the next, rising to a crescendo and then falling to a trickle before the same nervous tension commands silence once more as I feel the watering of my eyes as I hold my cheers inside.

The presentation came to an end.

I nailed that round of applause that I have pictured myself having. I gazed deep through the auditorium one last time. I saw Taurus in the back seat of the room smiling at me while I smiled back at him.

Today I had the same smile I had in my 14th story balcony.

Today, I overcame my long resting fears.

Today, I broke through my jail, which I had thought was real for so long that I never even checked to see if the walls were solid. I heard screams from other cells, and they paralyzed me from even pushing on the door. But when the brilliant light of dawn shone in, I stood and put my hand on the bars. With a prayer, I pushed with all my might, and after a brief flash of pain, the prison cell itself was left behind me on a hill. From the outside, it was tiny, pathetic. After so long crouched in the dark, I stood up and let the light warm my skin, my black hair flowing in a heavenly wind. Upon the walls written in stone were the words.

"Stutter"

"Fear."

"Taurus."

I threw my head toward the sky with relief. All I had to do was conquer those bullies all along, conquer them and be free.

Today, I finally destroyed 'The Tongue Chains.'

Chapter 15
A Letter to Stutter (Optional)

They say that worry ends when faith begins.

That day, faith found its way through me. I know you probably think I didn't stutter in my last speech. In fact, I did, but no one ever noticed. They didn't notice for several reasons, the audience were too drawn to the subject itself that they didn't want to pay attention to something that is so shallow, I was so into what I am saying and presenting rather than being mentally indulged in that endless abyss of "how am I going to say the next word." it's a mental state I've wanted to achieve since a very long time.

It maybe is a small thing for normal people, a regular achievement for many, but it's not for me, and it never was. Maybe if you look at the world from a stutterer's eyes, you'll know it's not.

Don't ever underestimate what we're going through, what we have encountered in our lives, how people view us, and if you ever crossroads with a stutterer, know you're standing in front of a hero, a warrior who has been fighting wars silently trying to prove himself, or rather trying to survive in a ruthless and cruel community.

I believe every person who stutters has their own unique story and different feelings about stuttering. I hope that all people (stutterers and non-stutterers) can use each other's stories to build the confidence that they deserve to have.

Approximately five percent of all children go through a period of stuttering that lasts six months or more. Three-quarters of those will recover by late childhood, leaving about one percent with a long-term problem, affecting four times as many males as females. Some of us find ways to attain fluency; some of us don't. Until now, there are no instant miracle cures for stuttering. Therapy, electronic devices, and even drugs are not an overnight process. However, a specialist in stuttering can help not only children but also teenagers, young adults, and even older adults make good progress toward fluency.

Normally, children and adults who stutter are no more likely to have psychological or emotional problems than children and adults who do not. Some say there is no reason to believe that emotional trauma causes stuttering. Some say the opposite. In my case am not sure if it was the dream that caused it, but surprisingly after so many years, for some reason, I can't seem to forget it.

Brothers and sisters worldwide, accept your stutter. Never stop working on yourself, for letting yourself drown in the zone of despair is painful.

If you're a teenager, your life at some point might convey an impression of hollowness, it's dark, and you can't get out, it's okay, it is normal, you'll get past this, just don't let it eat you alive.

Educate yourself, be the best version of yourself and always remember that *true knowledge is power, power is confidence, and confidence is the key to fluency.*

Talk! Don't ever let being afraid to stutter stop you from talking or expressing yourself. Speak out just whatever you want to say without ever thinking about the consequences. You'll be amazed how fluent words will come out, although you thought you'd stutter in every single word.

If there are some tips to reduce stuttering, I've learned throughout my journey. It is to always maintain eye contact with everyone as you'll often find yourself breaking eye contact with the person you're speaking to, which is normal. This stems from the anxiety associated with stuttering. Even if you start stuttering, force yourself to maintain eye contact. This action makes you look more confident, and building up your own confidence will help reduce your stutter over time. If you do end up breaking eye contact, just regain it as you try to stop stuttering.

Also, making hand motions can sometimes come in handy as Stuttering is sometimes the result of nervous energy that your body doesn't know what to do with making hand motions channels this energy elsewhere. This can distract your brain from the stutter and help you speak smoothly. This technique is especially useful if you give a public presentation.

And remember to always keep your Taurus controlled. The mere thought of surrendering will instantly recall stuttering to your speech, always keep your confidence levels up, your ignorance for stuttering always active as this is perhaps the only paths out there to overcome stuttering, maybe temporary, some will overcome it forever if this was truly mastered.

In the journey to fluency, if you're a stutterer, you'll notice by now that you pass through phases, just like everything in life, ups, and downs, some days you feel yourself so caring free for what people think, more like a sudden boost of confidence, you could narrate stories without even thinking about stuttering which would normally as well lead to minimal or almost a fluent speech, other days you'll have some intense stuttering. In both ways, it will always be there, and take it or not, you will have to live with it.

Too many times, I tend to stutter in front of people I used to know a long time ago upon meeting again after a long break. Deep inside, I want to show them that I don't stutter anymore. Today, I could care less about that.

Every stutterer and even non-stutterer has his own triggers toward motivation. In my case, my trigger was my own enemy, Taurus. I never settled for a talk-less job, or even a talk-less medical specialty like many people advised me to, including the person who loved me the most, my mother.

I am a multilingual stutterer speaking six totally different languages, English, French, Russian, German, Arabic, and Ukrainian.

In my life, I chose jobs like a seller, a waiter, a taxi driver, a trainer, a salesman, a cook, a coach, and finally, a surgeon. Most of the times, I come to intentionally put myself in places that I was obliged to talk, rather than settling for other jobs, just for the reason that I refuse to let my disability lead my future to places where I don't want to go anymore, or maybe order food that I don't want to. I rather chose the most difficult and challenging jobs a stutterer could have just to prove a point to myself, to my enemies, and finally to the world.

Chase your dreams. Even if they seem too far away, you can be the next number one Hollywood actor, a worldwide known speaker, or even the next president. And just in case you didn't know, there are thousands of successful stutterers out there including and not limited to Emily Blunt, James Earl Jones, John Stossel, Bill Walton, Mel Tillis, Winston Churchill, Marilyn Monroe, Carly Simon, Annie Glenn, Ken Venturi, Bob Love, John Updike, King George VI, and many more. All are famous people who stuttered and went on to have successful lives.

There was a time when I used to sit alone and keep on imagining my life without stuttering, creating stories about how better and easier it would have been. Now, I also sit alone, imagining the same thing, just to realize I was wrong. My stutter created me; it created the person I am today. It gave me a lot of tools to stand and be heard despite all the odds. As much as I hated it at some points in my life, I will forever be grateful for it.

It may have taken me a bit longer than I wanted, but today I can say that I embrace and accept my stutter. While I may still have days when my speech is more troublesome than normal, and I become dissatisfied, I know that I wouldn't be who I am today without my stutter. I wouldn't have the work ethic and confidence that I have built up if I wasn't faced with this challenge. My stutter has forced me into situations that I never thought I could handle.

I remember the days I prayed for what I have today. I remember the past and reflect on some of the supports and roadblocks throughout my years, all of us have different roads we must take, different interests and goals that we seek, but determination and perseverance help us achieve all of our goals. I have a job that I love, in a place where I'm happy to call my home with friends, family, and a wonderful wife, who all combine to make life more than I could have ever imagined.

Things can and will get better. It may take a lifetime, but don't give up. Your life is worth fighting for. One final thought; it is okay to stutter; accepting that fact, along with teaching others, is something I will strive for throughout my career.

Me, at the end of the day, I am just another stutterer in this big world, and this is just my little big story.

Chapter 16
New Horizons

Every finish line is the beginning of a new race.

I Woke up today with a new dream, more like a vision, a hope to find a real cure for stuttering.

As I've done my research in neurosurgery and reading about how the cerebral blood flow can affect the superior speech cortex and how it affects the brain's physiology leading to stuttering. I got accepted abroad as my journey is about to dawn in another country as a doctor/researcher in a university far away from my home in a country known for good cheese and expensive watches, Switzerland.

I went to visit dad and Nour's grave one last time before my plane takes off.

As the bodies of the beloved return their matter to the earth, their souls, ageless since birth, return to our maker. I let my feet tread lightly over the soils that support new spring growth, white-bells and green wands of grass, until I am there, my eyes resting on their names, my heart hearing the sound of their voices as if they were right there with me. Perhaps it is the memories that are the real bridge, that sense of love a key to open doors into the worlds beyond, yet here I am in the graveyard, these moments of reflection our everlasting bond. I drop a flower, recite a prayer, and take the highway to the airport.

With Taurus sitting next to me in the front seat, ready for all the highs and lows I am about to face.

The question is, are you ready for the next ride?

THE END

This is a tribute to Ukraine, my favourite city and my second home, Vinnytsia.

Its tearing and heart breaking to witness what's happening there right now.

I stand for you and by you, as you were and are a part of me and you will always be.

They will never destroy the memories, affection, love and impact you have put in my mind and heart.

May the war stop and may god grant you peace, the peace you deserve.

Slava Ukraina.

CPSIA information can be obtained
at www.ICGtesting.com
Printed in the USA
BVHW051920200323
660799BV00011B/154